Marilyn

MARILYN

DIVA. GODDESS. WOMAN.

Text by
Chiara Pasqualetti Johnson

whitestar

Contents

*Marilyn Monroe in 1956, at the peak of her splendor.
The platinum hair, languid expression, and lipstick-coated smile
were key to turning the Hollywood star into an icon.*

Introduction

Marilyn the goddess. She needs no last name as her first one is enough to evoke the myth of the world's most famous woman. Her image has become so unmistakable, frequently imitated, and artfully reworked that it's almost impossible to imagine that someone that famous could ever have existed. Her face is absolutely iconic, at least as much as Leonardo da Vinci's *Mona Lisa*. Like the latter, she is forever smiling. Yet for all that, she wasn't a happy person. And it may be in precisely that mysterious sadness that the secret of her never-faltering charm lies. Complex, profound, tormented, and gorgeous, she had all the ingredients required of a legend, starting with her double identity: that of the obscure Norma Jeane who transformed herself into the divine Marilyn Monroe without ever casting aside the dark shadows of her past. Beneath the sparkling patina of her success, she remained forever a fragile child, marked by an unhappy childhood, fatherless and deserted by her mother. An immense loss, a dreadful void, a sense of abandonment that left her wounded for good. She did all she could to shake off the sad memories of her tumultuous beginnings. She changed her name and allowed photographers, directors, and producers to transform her into a hot, desirable object, but never forgot that hers was a fragile soul. And this soul suffered each time she got burned or had to put up with uncalled-for malice. As a girl, she had been aware of the misery that lay hidden behind the scintillating Hollywood dream machine. She had taken on a titanic struggle to become a better self. An insecure perfectionist, she worked hard to shape her image, bending to the demands of scripts that she simultaneously embody the goddess of love and the girl next door. The result of all this effort was a magical alchemy, a perfect blend of vulnerability and sensuality. But whoever believes that success was the sole objective of that relentless ascent is terribly mistaken. "She wanted not to be famous, but to be a good and appreciated actress," claimed Lee Strasberg, the grand master of the Actors Studio, at which Marilyn honed her talent.

A public relations photo for the launch of Niagara. *It was the snapshots from this series that Andy Warhol used to create his legendary silkscreen prints of Marilyn.*

Marilyn the diva. She dreamt of winning an Oscar, an honor that never came her way. Her career was meteoric, lasting only sixteen years, during which she established herself as an actress, producer, singer, entrepreneur, and, above all, sex symbol. Far from aspiring to Hollywood's ideal of the modest and sensible woman of the 1950s, she played the part of the "dumb blonde" to perfection. In real life, however, she was anything but naive. She may have appeared frivolous and inane, but she wasn't in the least. She transformed clothing and makeup into tools of seduction: a white, circular skirt that flew up when the subway passed; diamonds as allegedly her best friends; a fake mole at the side of her mouth, its sex appeal heightened by a swipe of lipstick; platinum hair; two drops of Chanel N°5 before climbing into bed. She became the epitome of Hollywood stardom, but also of the new female image. And it was precisely in this that her contribution to the realm of style lay: freely enjoying her sexuality, she harnessed femininity and made it powerful. It's no coincidence that her success coincided with the epochal changes of the late 1950s. Thanks to a temperament capable of revolutionizing the rules, Marilyn, like Elvis and rock 'n' roll, marked an irreversible turning point in popular morality, both on and off the set.

Marilyn the woman. In sync with the characters she played on screen, Marilyn got herself involved in multiple tumultuous and impossibly complicated romantic relationships. Hers is a story of tormented affairs and unborn children, dominated by burning passions that consumed her soul. Any descent into the abyss she had to deal with almost entirely on her own, suspended between her unstoppable triumph on screen and her desperate failure in the private sphere. At the mere age of sixteen, she married the son of a neighbor, only to land in the solid arms of Joe DiMaggio, the legendary baseball player of the New York Yankees, in a marriage brandished on the front page of every tabloid. Hounded by paparazzi, she later wed the playwright Arthur Miller amid circulating rumors of other affairs—real

Marilyn seated on a sidewalk retouching her makeup in the early 1950s. The book next to her is Mabel Elsworth Todd's The Thinking Body, *a manual on human physiology.*

or presumed—above all, with U.S. president John F. Kennedy. She became the symbol of an era and every man's illicit dream even if all she really wanted was a protective hug. She did not live long enough to find the love of her dreams. Her premature death, shrouded in mystery and subject to endless speculation, helped turn her into an icon, crystallized in the eternal present through thousands of pictures. The most famous of these repeat the stereotype: a mouth half-open and eyes half-closed, as if in the throes of ecstasy. But it is the lesser known ones that tell the true story of Marilyn, the one hidden behind the glamorous mask. Brought together on the pages of this book are over 120 photographs, chosen over the course of extensive research to capture the star from a different perspective: that of her poignant humanity.

While writing this book I often asked myself what Marilyn's life would have been like had she had a family that truly loved her, and had she not been forced to start from the very bottom. I also wondered how a woman like her would have responded to the #MeToo movement were she alive today. Who knows if she would have stooped so low as to compromise with photographers, directors, and producers, as was the custom in her time. Who knows if she would have managed to reconcile her career with a family, as she had so dreamed of doing—and as we all still dream of doing today since although many things have changed since then, others have remained the same. For years, those who wrote about Marilyn were primarily men, many of whom still clung to outdated notions and sexist stereotypes.

This also explains why "Marilyn Monroe" and "feminism" rarely appear in the same sentence. Yet Marilyn did challenge Hollywood to an epic battle, breaking her contract with Twentieth Century-Fox to found her own production company.

Marilyn in a meadow in Palm Springs, California, in 1953.

And though she did not live to see the changes she had wrought, she forever changed the rules of the game. Buckling under the strain of her own beauty, she seemed unrefined but was, in fact, attracted to music, poetry, and politics. She was also an avid reader, one who poured her thoughts out on paper. This is also why I, while researching Marilyn's life, have preferred to draw directly on her own words in interviews and personal testimony that appears in her own writing and in her autobiography, *My Story*, which she completed with the help of a professional ghostwriter, Ben Hecht, the screenwriter of movies like *Notorious* and *Some Like It Hot*. On these pages, truth and fiction intertwine in a complex jumble that Marilyn herself made extremely difficult to unravel as she sought the path that led to success.

Forever suspended between ambition and modesty, she reflected on the dangers of fame in her final interview. "It's nice to be included in people's fantasies, but you also like to be accepted for your own sake," she noted. But who, in actual reality, was Marilyn Monroe? To find her, I tried to look beyond my biases and force myself to tell her story nonjudgmentally. I ask all of you to do the same as you leaf through this book. To catch a glimpse of the real Marilyn, you need to set aside the image of both the goddess and the star and allow yourself to be surprised by the woman who she was. Intelligent, determined, exceptionally talented, and endowed with an extraordinary sense of humor. A restless, independent, fragile, and mysterious soul. A myth for all time to come.

The actress in a public relations image shot by Ted Baron in the mid-1950s.

On the following page, sheathed in a black sequin gown, Marilyn Monroe poses for one of her most famous portraits, shot by Richard Avedon in New York in May 1957.

"The happiest time
of my life is now.
As far as I'm concerned,
I have a future and can't
wait to make it happen."

On the previous pages, an iconic photograph shot by Kirk Douglas on November 17, 1961. The star died eight months later.

Marilyn on a tiger skin rug as photographed by Richard Avedon in 1957. The image was used to promote the movie The Prince and the Showgirl.

How a Star Was Born

Norma Jeane was a shy child, scarred by her mother's abandonment. All this changed after she decided to turn her back on a childhood spent between orphanages and foster families so that she could pursue her dream of working in the movie industry. Dyeing her brown locks platinum, she became Marilyn Monroe, her name and life forever changed.

"Every child needs a father," sang Marilyn Monroe in one of her first roles, that of a dancer in search of true love in *Blonde Orchid*. Like a chick that nobody taught how to fly, she had grown up without the care of loving parents, thrown about from one foster family and orphanage to another. Her childhood had been a painful muddle of dreams and sorrows, insecurity and loneliness, resilience and desperation—a prelude to a life as dazzling as it was tormented.

Norma Jeane was first abandoned when she was only two weeks old. Shortly after giving birth, Gladys Monroe realized that she was utterly unfit to be a mother despite having already borne two other children. These she had entrusted to her first husband, Newton Baker, a salesman whom she had married at the age of fifteen. That marriage had been short-lived, however, and as soon as the divorce went through, Gladys moved to Hollywood, where she got a job in one of the labs that powered the flourishing movie industry. Wearing white gloves, she cut negatives for Consolidated Film Industries, spending hours on images that would entertain millions of Americans.

It was during her long days in the laboratory that she became friends with Grace McKee, with whom she ended up sharing a tiny apartment and the dream of every girl back in those times: to look like the movie stars who walked by their workbench each day.

One of the earliest known photos of Norma Jeane, who was born on June 1, 1926.

Baby Norma Jeane, several months after her birth, in the arms of her mother, Gladys.

REGISTRATION DISTRICT NO. 1901 **CERTIFIED COPY OF BIRTH RECORD** REGISTRAR'S NUMBER 7791

NAME OF CHILD—FIRST NAME	MIDDLE NAME	LAST NAME
NORMA	JEANE	MORTENSON
SEX	DATE OF BIRTH—MONTH DAY YEAR	
FEMALE	Jun. 1, 1926	
PLACE OF BIRTH—CITY OR TOWN		PLACE OF BIRTH—COUNTY
LOS ANGELES		LOS ANGELES
MAIDEN NAME OF MOTHER		COLOR OR RACE
GLADYS MONROE		WHITE
NAME OF FATHER		COLOR OR RACE
EDWARD MORTENSON		WHITE
DATE RECEIVED BY LOCAL REGISTRAR	DATE(S) OF CORRECTION(S), IF ANY	
Jun. 5, 1926		

This is to certify, that the foregoing is a true and correct copy of statements appearing on the record of birth of the above named child, as filed in this office

SIGNATURE OF CERTIFYING OFFICIAL	
George M. Uhl, M.D.	Health Officer & Registrar
PLACE OF CERTIFICATION	DATE CERTIFIED
LOS ANGELES, CALIFORNIA	Oct. 24, 1955

STATE OF CALIFORNIA REV. 7-1-49 FORM R85-61 DEPARTMENT OF PUBLIC HEALTH

The child's original birth certificate, issued by the State of California, in which she's registered as Norma Jeane Mortenson.

For a split second, she thought she had discovered true joy with a young worker of Norwegian origin, Edward Mortenson, whom she married in 1924. The dream lasted only a few months, and a year later, when she learned that she was pregnant, Gladys found herself alone again. She wasn't even sure of the father's identity, as it could have been any of the guys she was hanging out with at the time.

Norma Jeane Mortenson was born on June 1, 1926. On her birth certificate from the Los Angeles General Hospital, Gladys Monroe, her mother, declared her ex-husband the father and assigned the newborn his surname. She immediately made it clear that she did not want to take care of the child. As she had already proven in the past, Gladys was incapable of providing her children with the attention and emotional stability that she herself had never received. She was also terrified at the possibility that she had inherited the mental illness that ran in her family. Both her mother and father had spent the final years of their lives in psychiatric institutions, while her brother suffered from paranoid schizophrenia, a diagnosis that reinforced Gladys's belief that her family was doomed to suffer from mental disorders. She thus decided to entrust Norma Jeane to the Bolenders, a married couple in California. Like other families of the time, they supplemented their income through payments they received for taking in foster children. Dedicated members of one of the many Catholic congregations that flourished early in the century, they viewed education as a mission and punished any sign of lack of virtue with severity.

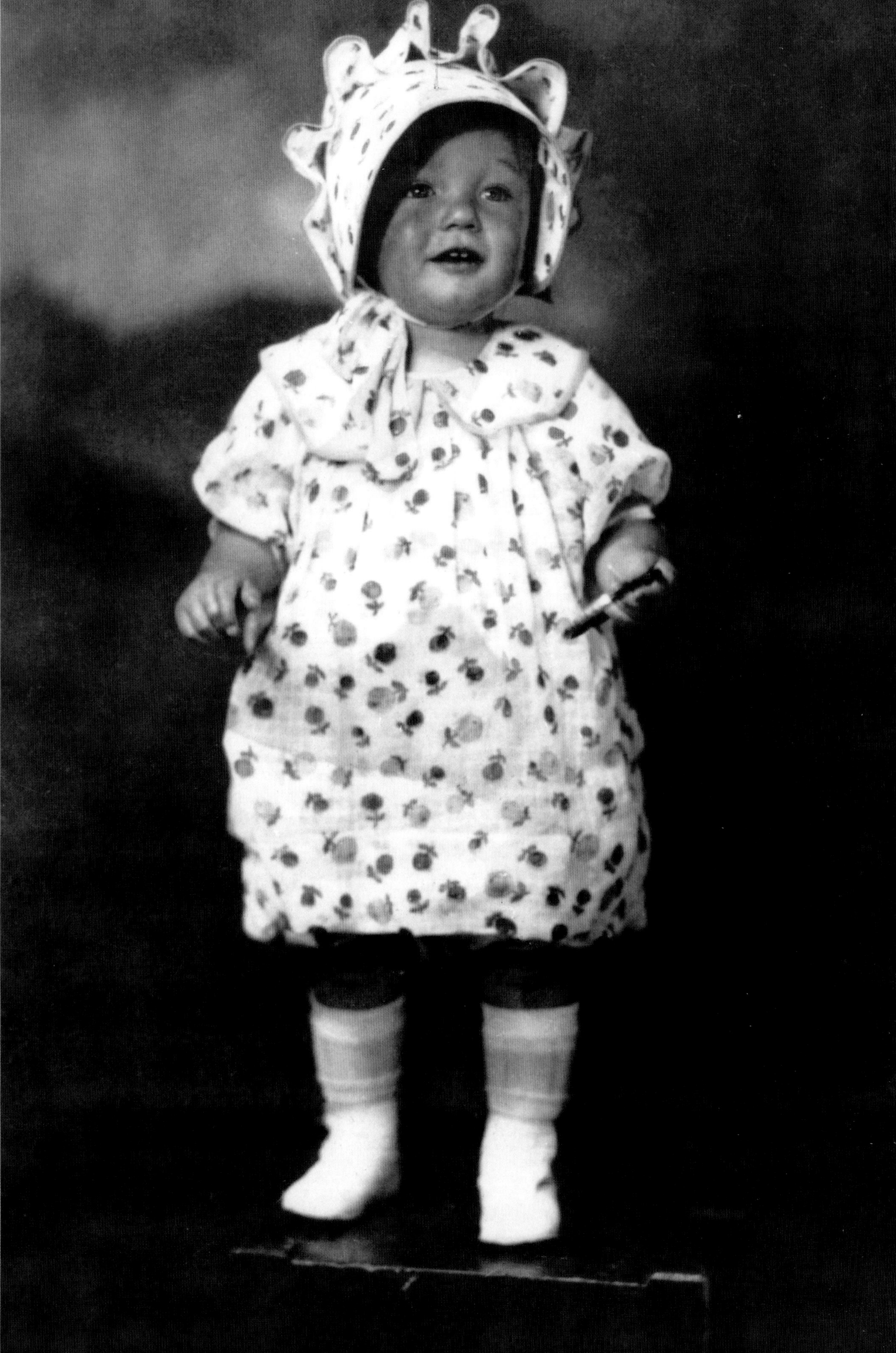

They regarded smoking, playing cards, and any form of entertainment as inconceivable vices. "We are people who go to church, not the movies," they explained to the little girl, warning her of the dangers posed by the immoral tales promoted by the movie industry.

Norma Jeane remained with the family for seven years, sharing a modest four-room home with other children. Occasionally her mother dropped by and took her to picnics on the shore, where she could mingle with the happy families who mobbed Sunset Beach on Saturdays. Her few childhood photographs show a child with a shy smile and bright eyes framed by ash-blonde locks. Behind her bright mien, Norma Jeane was hiding the shadows of emotional fragility caused by the fleeting apparition of a woman who asked her to call her "Mommy" for a few hours before vanishing once again. "She didn't come very often," she later recalled. "To me she was simply the lady with red hair."

During those brief visits, Gladys would tell her that her absent father, whose portrait hung on the child's bedroom wall, was a man as handsome as Clark Gable. Gazing at him, Norma Jeane dreamt that one day he would return. This was the beginning of a lifelong fantasy, a chase after someone she could call "Daddy."

For a long time Norma Jeane had to settle on a father figure that existed only in her imagination, though eventually she realized that the man actually existed. It was only many years later, when she was already a movie star, that she succeeded in tracking him down. He went by the name Charles Stanley Gifford. "I discovered his name and many other things about him, that he once lived in the same apartment building as my mother, that they fell in love and that he left at the time I was born without ever having seen me," she recounted. Meanwhile she did everything possible to get him to meet her at least once. Yet, the father about whom she had dreamt so long remained a faceless shadow. Rejecting all her entreaties, he destroyed any possibility of establishing a bond and thus condemned his daughter to a sorrow impossible to alleviate. His absence left an invisible wound that deeply marked Norma Jeane's relationships with men, leaving her with scars that never fully healed.

A photo portrait of Norma Jeane at age two.

On the top, Norma Jeane and her mother, Gladys, at the beach in 1929.

On the right, at age five, grinning while posing on a wooden chair, flaunting that irresistible smile that would one day make her famous.

At the age of seven, Norma Jeane was returned to the custody of her biological mother. They moved into a furnished house that they shared with a couple of British actors, not far from the movie studios where Gladys worked. Here, dinner conversations almost always revolved around the movies and were spiked with celebrity gossip, cigarette smoke, and whiskey shots. Nothing could have been further from the dull evenings that Norma Jeane had spent with her foster family. "They drank, they played cards, they sang. Given my religious upbringing, I was shocked. I thought they were all going to hell. I spent hours praying for them," she recalled. All of a sudden, cinema was no longer sinful, but a harmless pastime that provided a living for families like theirs.

Norma Jeane spent hours fantasizing about a different life, imagining herself as greatly loved, desirable, and splendid as the stars she saw on screen. The movies became her refuge, her escape. She understood that the only way to survive an unhappy reality was to reinvent herself as someone else—someone the world would adore.

The seeming normality of life at the side of her real mother lasted only a brief time. Suffering from bouts of severe depression followed by angry outbursts, Gladys spent days in bed, consuming alcohol and drugs that, instead of calming her, altered her unstable character even more. Laid low by her illness, she succumbed to an irreversible spiral, so much so that in 1934 she was admitted to a psychiatric hospital—a refuge from a dark and lonely world from which she emerged less and less frequently. Save some brief interludes, she remained institutionalized until the time she died, many years after her daughter's demise. For Norma Jeane, she was a vague presence, an echo of endless pain. "She never made any attempt to be with me. I don't believe I ever existed for her."

Norma Jeane in 1933 playing with puppies. Even as a child, she adored animals and, over the course of her life, had many dogs. Her favorite was Mugsy, a collie she received as a gift at the time of her first marriage.

Love seemed to slip from her hands as, for the third time in her short life, Norma Jeane found herself confronting a new life along with a new mother figure. This time the child was taken in by Grace McKee, the friend who had shared secrets and dreams with Gladys. Abounding in curiosity, lively, and generous, she was to have a significant impact on the future star's life. Her job at a Hollywood dream factory had made her used to seeing the era's stars pass through her fingers as she snipped away the shots in which they appeared less glamorous in order to draw attention to those in which their natural beauty was enhanced by shadows, lights, and filters. As Grace could not bear children, she poured her affection and ambitions into her friend's daughter. Her concern for Norma Jeane's education and well-being was genuinely heartfelt, and she passed her own shattered dreams of becoming famous onto her. She dressed her up and styled her hair with care, convinced that she would become a movie star. "It was only later that I realized how much she had done for me," the actress wrote in her memoirs. Once again, however, Norma Jeane had to face the disappointment of a broken promise. Grace unexpectedly fell for a younger man—already a father to three girls—whom she quickly wed in Las Vegas. He convinced her to get rid of the little girl, whom he considered a burden on their new life together.

Norma Jeane was thus forced to deal with yet another relationship that had come to an abrupt end. With tears in her eyes, she packed her bags and moved to an orphanage in Los Angeles. Donning a uniform, she became guest No. 3463. For two years she conformed to the military regime of the institution, which taught the children responsibility by providing them with a monthly allowance in exchange for performing minor tasks suited to their age. Norma Jeane's favorite pastime now became inventing new characters and imagining fantasy lives. "As a child, I did nothing but daydream. Even when I had to serve tables, I would imagine myself working as a maid in an elegant home," she recalled.

In her memoirs, she would transform this period into a nightmare of abuse and suffering that did not quite match the reality. On Saturdays, she would go out with Grace, her legal guardian, who would take her to the movies and afterward stop at a tea room or one of Hollywood's many beauty salons, where she taught her how to apply eyeliner and powder to enhance her pre-pubescent beauty. Grace also paid for the institution's annual fees and bought clothing for the child. Yet despite all this, Norma Jeane knew she could not count on her presence. Occasionally, Grace skipped the Saturday visit, reducing the little girl to utter despair. "In that period, I was not used to being happy."

Norma Jeane at age nine in a colored-photo headshot that shows off her eyes and lips.

A very young Norma Jeane at the beach in Avalon on Catalina Island.

On the right, Norma Jeane with a group of friends at a Chinese restaurant in 1942. Sitting next to her and visible on the right is Grace McKee.

Two years later, Grace convinced her husband to take the girl into their home. What seemed like a return to family life once again proved to be an illusion. Norma Jeane remained in her new home for only a few months. Her stay came to an abrupt halt after Grace's husband, attempting to molest Norma Jeane, roughly caressed her while drunk. Her first physical contact with a man thus transformed what should have been a tender gesture into violence, divorcing love from sex forever in the child's mind. Grace's solution was to move the girl far away and entrust her to a distant relative, Aunt Ana, yet another surrogate mother. This time, however, the choice proved a happy one. A plump woman with white hair, Ana Lower was extroverted and generous. The period the two spent together was a peaceful interlude in the little girl's life. She finally had a home to which she could return, where someone who loved her awaited her. "She never gave me any grief, not once. She couldn't have. She was all kindness and love."

When asked in school who her real parents were, Norma Jeane gave evasive answers, distorting a reality that was too difficult for a child her age to grasp. She claimed that her mother was dead and that her father was living in Europe. "I lied because I was ashamed to let the world know that I had been born out of wedlock and had never heard the voice of my estranged father." She continued doing so even after she became a star and ended up turning the poignant image of an abandoned child into a badge of honor. During interviews, she fabricated stories, dramatizing her childhood memories with fanciful tales. The twelve adoptive homes, the thrashings, the hunger, her grandmother's attempt to suffocate her with a pillow, and the hints of a possible sexual assault she had suffered as a child were legends that she herself fueled in order to win the sympathy of the press. Her unhappy past had an impact on the public, which she exploited in every conceivable way. All the same, it was definitely based on a reality through which she had actually lived, and the years of her childhood were marked by a pain she would never forget. "This sad and bitter little girl, who grew up too quickly has a hard time disappearing from my heart. Despite her success, I can still feel her frightened eyes peering out of mine."

On the left, a fifteen-year-old Norma Jeane posing for her first advertisement.

On the right, a photo portrait from the same period.

By 1939, Norma Jeane had blossomed. At thirteen, she reached her adult height of five foot six, and her figure began to assume the shape that would make her famous. With skirts wrapped snugly around her hips and cardigans showing off her budding breasts, she crossed the street on her way to school with workers whistling after her. All of a sudden, she was no longer invisible, and the world began to feel like a nice place.

Thanks to Grace's instruction, she knew how to use cosmetics effectively and style her brown curls by running her fingers through her tresses. She began wearing slacks, provoking outrage among her teachers and rousing the admiration of her classmates. Although she longed to be looked at, she knew how to play the role of the good girl. She never gave rise to gossip and was considered fairly shy by her friends. For all that, she was aware of her growing popularity and her power to seduce. "The truth is that, despite my lipstick, my mascara, and my precocious curves, I was as emotionless as a fossil. But apparently I made a certain impression on people," she said with surprise, thinking back on her adolescence. She thus decided that the moment had come for her to find a way to quit feeling like an orphan. This she did, at age sixteen, by getting married.

Her choice fell on Jim Dougherty, a neighbor and young mechanic who asked her for her hand in marriage several months after meeting her. Without her mother beside her and trembling like a leaf, she clung to her husband's arm and flashed a radiant smile on her wedding day. The young couple moved in together while the war was in full swing. In 1944, when Jim was sent to fight on the Pacific front, Norma Jeane moved in with her mother-in-law and found work in an airplane factory, where she spent all day spraying foul-smelling paint on metal fuselage. It was in this factory that a crew assigned to document the women's war effort noticed her. Its members were not looking for the usual propagandistic images, but rather for pretty girls happy to show the world their patriotic contributions. Among the photographers was David Conover, who shot a series of portraits of Norma Jeane, in which she appears on the assembly line with a dazzling smile, her large eyes wide open, and her brown locks tossed back. It was he who suggested that she apply to Blue Book, the modeling agency run by the formidable Emmeline Snively, with whom a contract meant seeing the doors to a golden world spring open.

Norma Jeane was hired as a model, though it soon became clear that this line of work wasn't for her. What she did best was look sexy in advertisements. Within a few months, she had appeared on dozens of women's magazine covers, where it was she, not what she was wearing, that roused interest. Once she completed a shoot, she would meticulously inspect each photograph. With her inquisitive eye, she would study the images for hours, lingering over the expressions that she didn't like in order to understand what she had done wrong and how she could improve.

With her first earnings, Norma Jeane was able to leave her job at the factory and the home of her mother-in-law. Just as she rented a room of her own, the agency put her in touch with a young photographer of Hungarian origin, André de Dienes. Famous for his portraits of movie stars such as Ingrid Bergman and Shirley Temple, he was looking for a model willing to pose, possibly nude, in out-of-door Wild West settings. Norma Jeane refused to pose without clothes, but she allowed herself to be seduced by this sweet and talented guy who began courting her from the moment he first laid eyes on her. "This adorable little girl walked in wearing a pink sweater and a pair of checked pants. I immediately fell in love," de Dienes recalled. He demonstrated—not only with words—that he regarded her sex appeal as irresistible, filling her with the confidence that she desperately needed.

Norma Jeane in 1948, still with long hair and the candor of a young girl but already posing like a professional. Her transformation into a movie star was to begin shortly thereafter.

Meanwhile, work with the agency continued going well. The form used to recommend Norma Jeane to photographers and advertisers noted her height, weight (115 pounds), measurements (30-24-32), blue eyes, perfect teeth, and brown hair, a color deemed too dark. She thus found herself sitting in the comfortable chairs of Frank & Joseph, one of Hollywood's most popular beauty salons, where she had her hair dyed a golden hue. Over time, it would be bleached to platinum. Indeed, her signature hairstyle, which required constant maintenance for the rest of her life, turned her into the most famous blonde in history.

Flaunting her new look, she found herself before a movie camera for the first time; wearing a bathing suit, she smiled and waved. Until that point, she had only taken part in a couple of school plays and had no experience as an actress. "I bore this secret within me, this desire to act," she said years later. When she filed for divorce from Dougherty in the summer of 1946, she had nothing but her dreams. He wanted a wife and children, she a career. They would never see each other again. Just as the the divorce papers came through, the news for which she had been waiting arrived. Twentieth Century-Fox wanted to cast her in a walk-on role. Although the pay was modest and the future uncertain, she was thrilled. The contract also came with a new name. The producers suggested that she take inspiration from Marilyn Miller, the star of the *Ziegfeld Follies*, a Broadway musical. To this she added her mother's maiden surname: Monroe. "Two M's will bring you luck," they promised. And so, August 1946 saw the birth of Marilyn Monroe.

Norma Jeane in a swimsuit on a California beach in 1948. She was among the first models to wear a bikini, the two-piece swimsuit considered so shamelessly "explosive" that it was named after the atoll in the Marshall Islands where the U.S. was conducting its nuclear tests.

"No one ever told me I was pretty when I was a little girl. All little girls should be told they're pretty, even if they aren't."

A splendid and very young Norma Jeane posing on the beach for a swimsuit photo early in her career.

Two shots of Norma Jeane by photographer Richard Miller in the mid-1940s, the first showing her in a swimming pool, the second, playing in the ocean.

The young actress posing in Los Angeles for photographer Earl Theisen right after signing her first contract with Twentieth Century-Fox. Recalling her first ventures into the movie business, she noted: "If other girls knew how terrible I was at the beginning, I'm sure they would take heart. Ultimately, I decided that I wouldn't let my lack of self-esteem get the better of me."

The Goddess of Hollywood

Insecure and a perfectionist, Marilyn patiently constructed her image as a movie star. Portrayed by the greatest photographers of the era and chased by swarms of paparazzi, she caused a sensation and roused admiration wherever she went. Shot after shot, her pin-up body lit up by her bright smile became the model of the new, modern beauty.

The movie theaters of Hollywood were grand palaces, veritable cathedrals of entertainment, adorned with stucco, marble, and fountains. It was in these fantasy temples that Marilyn, like millions of Americans, spent many happy hours letting her imagination run wild. Every Saturday morning she purchased a front-row seat from which she watched the screen with a single desire: that of becoming a star, just like those she admired in the movies. "I used to sit there all day long, right in front, where the screen was so large," she recalled. Her favorite actress was Jean Harlow, a passionate blonde with a hypnotic gaze. Irresistibly charming, she embodied the dream of a young woman who longed to be adored like a goddess. Her identification with the most scandalous and fascinating actress of the early talkies, who had died ten years earlier, seemed bold but proved to be far too simplistic.

At twenty-one, Marilyn had not yet gained recognition but was already paving her road to success. Making sure that she did not go unnoticed by the journalists and advertising agents who hung around the movie studios, she gained the sympathy of those in the industry while still a nobody. In early 1947, she was finally called on a set for a minor role as an extra in the movie *Scudda Hoo! Scudda Hay!* Nonetheless, this first performance landed almost entirely on the cutting-room floor. In the sole shot in which she is visible, she delivers a single line—"Hi, Rad"—as she greets the protagonist. A few months later, she was offered a small part in *Dangerous Years*, in which she played a waitress and spoke several lines. This time, however, her name appeared at the bottom of the credits, filling her with the sense that the movie business was her true calling.

On the top, Marilyn on the movie set of Scudda Hoo! Scudda Hay! *in 1947.*

On the bottom, a photo taken on the set of Dangerous Years, *which marked her first screen appearance as a waitress called Evie.*

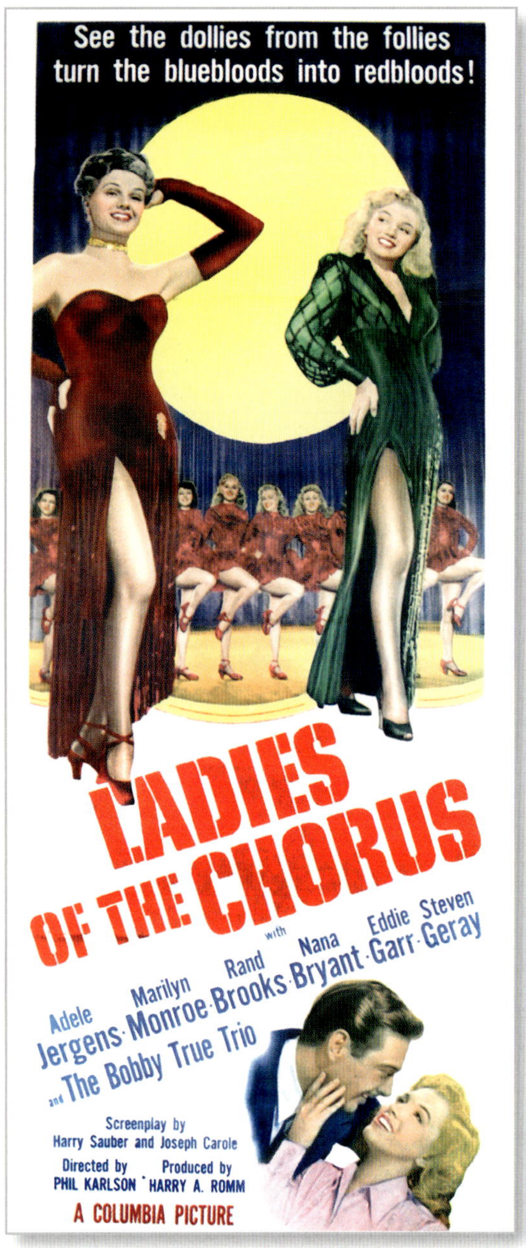

On the left, the poster for the movie Ladies of the Chorus.

On the right, Marilynpp at the center of the photo posing in a black dress during the filming of a musical number in the movie, in which she played Peggy Martin and sang "Every Baby Needs a Da Da Daddy."

Confirmation arrived soon afterward, when she got her first opportunity to speak, sing, and dance in *Ladies of the Chorus*, the type of second-rate movie that was shown in theaters after the principal one. This was the first in a series of scripts in which she played a character that seemed cut out for her—that of a girl from a poor home who pulls herself out of poverty and becomes a star.

In her role as Peggy, she played a vaudeville dancer used to the advances of wealthy men. Despite its mediocre script, the movie led to Marilyn's first review as an actress: "Among the best things in the picture are Miss Monroe's songs," wrote the *Motion Picture Herald*. Side by side with these words, came the first fan letters.

Actually, in those early years, Marilyn's fame lay more in photographs than in her fleeting appearances in the cinema. She became one of cartoonist and photographer Earl Moran's favorite pin-ups, and she posed for both Laszlo Willinger, the photographer famous for his shots of Marlene Dietrich and Hedy Lamarr, and Earl Theisen, who captured her wearing nothing but an empty "Ohio potatoes" sack, causing sales of the vegetable to soar. Some of these photographers became friends; others fell in love with the seductive creature flirting behind their lenses.

On the left, Marilyn, dressed in a potato sack, posing in a photograph for Earl Theisen in 1951. The photoshoot was a provocative response to a reporter's statement that the beauty of the young actress was due solely to the clothing she wore.

On the right, Marilyn in a swimsuit in the early 1950s.

Philippe Halsman, famous for his work for *Life* magazine, did multiple photoshoots of Marilyn over the years—first, in 1949, when she was only twenty-three years old. Immortalizing her in his iconic *Jumpology* series, he made her jump side by side with him. It was he, too, who was responsible for the famous cover of *Life* magazine in which Marilyn is portrayed wearing a white dress, with her shoulders bare, her eyes and lips half-closed in a pose simultaneously implying innocence and sensuality that was destined to become iconic. "Facing a man she didn't know, she only felt safe if she knew he desired her. Everything in her life was directed at rousing that desire," Halsman noted when speaking of her.

On the left, Marilyn jumping in one of the photos in Philippe Halsman's legendary Jumpology *series (1950s).*

On the top, the famous cover of a 1952 issue of Life *magazine that sealed the young actress's fate as a famous star.*

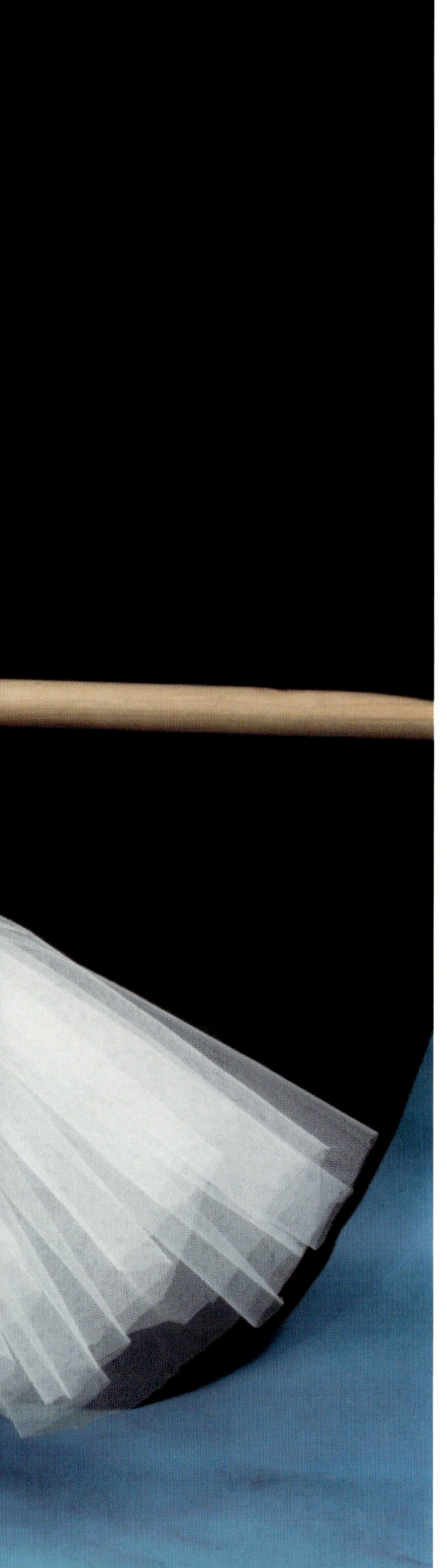

Of the many photographers, the most loyal was Milton Greene, whom Marilyn also took on as a partner when she decided to start a production company. Throughout her life, he tried to capture her soul more than her body. During one of their initial sessions, he made her wear his wife's large, black wool cardigan over her bare skin, then proceeded to shoot a sequence of memorable images. Many others followed, such as the famous *Ballerina* series, shot in a penthouse in New York, in which the actress wears a long white toile petticoat as she uses her arms to hold up the unlaced bodice that is too small to contain her curves. Likewise attracted to her was the female gaze of photographer Eve Arnold, who portrayed her absorbed in James Joyce's *Ulysses*.

A shot from the Ballerina *series taken by Milton Greene in 1954.*

How to develop your Thinking Ability
a guide to straight thinking and sound decisions
HOW TO DEVELOP YOUR THINKING ABILITY

It's no coincidence that various images capture Marilyn with a book in her hands. Unlike other movie stars, she actually enjoyed reading. Though she never did well at school, she learned how to appreciate literature and became an avid reader. The shelves in her living room were lined with novels by Thomas Wolfe, poems by Emily Dickinson, Flaubert's *Madame Bovary*, Whitman's *Leaves of Grass*, and the writings of Tolstoy, with bookmarks sticking out from between their pages. She had a note-filled anatomical textbook that she carefully studied in order to learn how the body works in motion, yet she also leafed through Sigmund Freud's *Interpretation of Dreams* searching for answers to her fears. Over time, she read Emerson's *Essays* and Edith Hamilton's *Greek Mythology*, George Sand's letters, and, while dreaming of becoming a dramatic actress, Nikolai M. Gorchakov's *Stanislavsky Directs*. The time she spent hanging out with journalists and critics—for romantic or other reasons—eventually left her library with 400 volumes. Thus Omar Khayyam's quatrains, the works of Edgar Allan Poe, and Kahlil Gibran's *Prophet* all ended up in her living room.

The genre that brought Marilyn the most immediate and spontaneous pleasure—unfiltered by scholarly criticism or learned discourse—was poetry. She knew Yeats's verses by heart, beginning with her favorite one: "All that is beautiful is but a brief, dreamy, tender pleasure." Such texts stoked her imagination, suggesting ideas and reflections. She filled her notebooks and diaries—discovered only after her death—with endless observations and short poems that revealed remarkable introspection. "I keep them all for my own sake. They're highly personal texts, that's it. They're full of my observations." The walls of her tiny apartment were adorned with cheap reproductions of works by Dürer, Fra Angelico, and Leonardo da Vinci, while a black-and-white photo of Eleonora Duse, an Italian diva of a previous era, stood on her night table. Eager to learn, she worked hard and approached life full force, bent on success.

The actress reading a book while lying in bed in her apartment at the Beverly Carlton Hotel, photographed by John Florea in the early 1950s.

"I was a blonde, but in my own way."

Although her career as a model was going smoothly, she was obsessed by the movies. She wore herself out with auditions; whenever she got nervous, a slight stammer caused her to stumble over her words and blush. Once the camera was whirring, however, her discomfort vanished, her hands grew steady, her movements fluid, and her radiant smile illuminated her beautiful face. Although she had little experience to fall back on, she knew how to exert charm. She had her irregular teeth straightened and underwent minor surgery to eliminate a tiny imperfection on her chin and slim down her nose. She applied her own makeup, emphasizing her lash line with eyeliner and adding a touch of color to make her eyebrows come to points and heighten her forehead. She used eyeshadow in delicate shades, based on the outfits she was wearing. Nail polish—fire-engine red or nude—was a must. The crowning touch was a sweep of coral lipstick.

Marilyn touching up her makeup during a filming on set. Eyeliner, red lipstick, and the famous mole on her lower cheek were key features of her look.

Promenade

Whenever Marilyn went shopping, she would shock the sales assistants by her reluctance to wear panties. On the other hand, she was obsessed with bras because a physician had told her that her breasts would remain high and firm if she always wore one. She thus wore them even at night and carefully chose the models that best fit her breasts. She also asked costume designers to insert buttons in the cups to emphasize her nipples, though she archly swore to the press that she wore nothing—absolutely nothing—beneath her clothing. "No underwear and no bustière. I like feeling free," she confided in interviews. Allegedly she devised a trick to make her gait sexier, cutting one of her heels by a quarter of an inch so that she would sway slightly while walking, thus making the sight of her derrière irresistible. It seems that it was precisely this manner of walking that won over Groucho Marx, who cast her in a sexy role in his movie *Love Happy*. This was the opportunity she had been waiting for. Although she appeared on screen for only a few seconds, the producers asked her to join a promotional tour to advertise the movie, certain that the presence of a sexy curvaceous blonde would draw in the public.

Marilyn with Groucho Marx on the set of Love Happy *in 1949.*

LH-144

Marilyn was fully aware that beauty could help a young actress like herself, but her greatest advantage lay in her desire to succeed, as she herself recollected: "When looking out into the night in Hollywood, I used to think: there must be millions of girls sitting by themselves like me, dreaming of becoming movie stars. But that doesn't matter: I dream harder than they do."

To improve her chances, she took classes at the Actor's Lab in Hollywood, an acting school behind Sunset Boulevard. "I wasn't under the slightest illusion that I was a good actress. I knew I was lousy. But what a will I had to learn!" she reminisced years later when recalling that period. What tormented her more than auditions was the desire for approval and her awareness that she lacked knowledge about culture. She therefore enrolled in a literature course at the University of California, Los Angeles, where she diligently attended classes dressed like any other student, with a pair of jeans from a department store and not a trace of makeup, so much so that none of her classmates suspected that she was an actress. She also took lessons from Mikhail Chekhov, nephew of the famous Russian playwright, who had studied under Stanislavsky and theorized his imagination- and movement-based method. When searching for instructors, she was generally attracted to intellectuals, father figures from whom she hoped to learn something. But, at that point in her life, the person who was providing her with the education that she needed was not a man, but a woman, namely, Natasha Lytess, a former actress who ran the acting classes at Columbia Pictures. Aristocratic and severe, she was known in the movie industry for her difficult personality and had a reputation for being a strict teacher. She was used to starlets with no talent, and when she first met Marilyn, that was precisely her impression. Yet though Marilyn was inhibited and clumsy, she was super enthusiastic and never missed a lesson. They worked together for months, during which time their bond shifted from that between student and teacher to that between friends. Natasha, in fact, became a mentor to the young woman and remained at her side for six years and through twenty-two movies.

The actress studying a script with Natasha Lytess, her acting coach, in the late 1950s.

Before long, Marilyn's effort was rewarded. She was signed on by Twentieth Century-Fox, which offered her a seven-year contract with a guaranteed salary of five hundred dollars per week plus a part in a major production, *The Asphalt Jungle*, a film noir directed by John Huston. Released in theaters in June 1950, it won the young star, who played the lover of an elderly criminal, recognition from critics. The *Times* mentioned her name and described her acting as "impeccable," while her photo appeared in *Life*.

Marilyn posing for a series of photos taken by Earl Theisen in her dressing room at Twentieth Century-Fox in November 1952.

On the top, a photo from the early 1950s taken in movie agent Johnny Hyde's garden in Beverly Hills.

On the right, a photograph by Earl Leaf of Marilyn reading a script.

On the following page, Marilyn auditioning for a part in a comedy at the Players Ring Theater in Los Angeles. Though she failed to get it, she was cast in a role in Asphalt Jungle, *one of her greatest hits, shortly thereafter.*

*"I want to be an artist,
not an erotic freak.
I don't want to be sold
to the public as a celluloid
aphrodisiac."*

Shortly afterward, she appeared on her first cover as an actress in *Look*, a distinguished magazine, and received a small part in a cinema history masterpiece, *All About Eve*. Sheathed in a white, strapless gown, she appeared in only two scenes and went nearly unobserved. The media, however, did take note of her presence, and *Photoplay* devoted an article to her entitled "How a Star Is Born."

Confirmation that her career was taking off came slightly later, during the filming of *Monkey Business* with Cary Grant. *Life* offered her its prestigious blessing, proclaiming, "Here, at last, is the real thing: a sensationally beautiful girl who has everything it takes to attract audiences to the box office from every corner of the world."

Gratified by these initial accolades, Marilyn wanted to prove that she could play more complex characters. For this reason, she happily accepted the challenge to take on a role in her first dramatic movie, *Don't Bother to Knock*. In it, she played Nell, a girl with a difficult childhood and raised in poverty, who, recently released from a psychiatric hospital, becomes dangerously destabilized after meeting a man who reminds her of her lost boyfriend. The part seemed written with her in mind, which may be why it made her so anxious. Helped by Natasha, she spent a long time preparing her performance, which everyone found convincing. Meanwhile, she began taking an interest in politics.

On the top, with the cast of All About Eve *(1950), directed by Joseph L. Mankiewicz.*

On the right, a photo of a scene used to promote the movie.

15

"If I'd observed all the rules, I'd never have got anywhere."

On the left, a scene from Monkey Business *with Cary Grant, the male lead.*

On the top, Marilyn with a chimpanzee during the shooting of the film in 1952.

On the following page, a black-and-white photo portrait taken by Slim Aarons in the early 1950s.

"I've played Marilyn Monroe, Marilyn Monroe, Marilyn Monroe. But she doesn't exist off screen. Off screen, I'm Norma Jeane."

She was keen to know what was going on in China, detested McCarthyism, and was firmly committed to the civil rights movement and the cause of African Americans. She decided to get directly involved in it after learning that Ella Fitzgerald, her favorite singer, could not get a gig at the Mocambo, the trendy club frequented by Hollywood stars. According to those who ran the venue, her physical appearance did not meet the criteria needed to perform on stage. Today, a friendship between a white and a black woman surprises no one, but at the time it represented an act of courage for both. The news that Marilyn had offered to attend all of Ella Fitzgerald's concerts at the Mocambo for a week, guaranteeing the club not only her own presence but that of other stars, caused a stir. On the night of Fitzgerald's debut, she sat in the front row, next to Frank Sinatra and Judy Garland.

Marilyn was fully aware of the hypocrisy of the puritanical and moralizing streak in American culture. She was exasperated by the country's social prejudices, above all when they were directed at her behavior. Although naive, she was not as naive as she let on. Rumors abounded that she was having affairs with producers and directors, but when a reporter asked her whether these were true, she replied with frankness: "They might be. But you don't become a star simply by sleeping with somebody. It takes a lot, lot more. Still, it helps." The crude way in which she had been sexually exploited by men in the movie industry was a subject about which she could be surprisingly candid throughout her life. After all, she had learned early on how to handle such men. "When I began modeling, it was basically part of the job. All the girls did it," she claimed in an interview. Hollywood was full of predators, and she was well aware of the rules of the game.

She hung out at fashionable clubs like the Romanoff in Beverly Hills, where she stood out for her cheerful laugh, jostling for attention among a crowd of gorgeous girls as eager as she was to land a part. Yet though she wore low-cut dresses that made her a sensation in that packed throng, she was not the usual arriviste. She appeared gentle and defenseless, so much so that practically everyone wanted to help her.

Marilyn with singer Ella Fitzgerald. The two were bound by a close friendship. In one interview the singer claimed, "I owe a great debt to Marilyn Monroe. She was an exceptional woman, a bit ahead of her time. And she didn't know it."

Indeed, Marilyn's seeming vulnerability eventually proved to be her greatest strength.

Around that time, a calendar from the past resurfaced in which Marilyn appeared scandalously naked. Its photos dated back to a time when, at age twenty-three, she had posed nude for Tom Kelley. During the shoot, she had insisted that the photographer's wife be present on the set, while her favorite album, Cole Porter's *Begin the Beguine*, resounded in the background.

Stretched out on the ground atop a red velvet drape, Marilyn radiated an explosive mix of voluptuousness and innocence. Within several years, these images had been taped all over the walls of garages and barber shops across the United States. It didn't take long for the press to connect the forms of this woman with the lovely face of the new star. Paralyzed by the ever more stringent moral censorship imposed by Senator McCarthy, the movie producers of the time had no idea how to handle the situation. Marilyn decided to shock everyone with the truth. Instead of exhibiting embarrassment, she shared with journalists her memories of the time when she had been a penniless, desperate girl, and thus transformed the scandal into a publicity stunt. Public opinion took an abrupt turn, and she was inundated by a flood of compassion.

Marilyn caught at a party in the mid-1950s.

Suddenly her life was the perfect embodiment of the American dream. "I appeared in a calendar. I don't want to be there for only a few; I want to be there for many—for the type of people from whom I come. I want a man, who gets home after a hard day's work, to look at this image and say: 'wow.'" The shots soon became more iconic than those of any other female nude in the history of photography. Notwithstanding the censorship of the period, they never stopped circulating, and even ended up on the cover of a new magazine founded in 1953. Called *Playboy*, it presented the scandalous images of Marilyn Monroe in its centerfold, proclaiming her the first, legendary Playmate.

Proud of her body, Marilyn considered nudity natural. "I'm comfortable only in the nude," she declared to a reporter. Sex, too, had stopped being taboo for her. "We're all sexual creatures from birth, thank God," she claimed while posing casually in skimpy bathing suits or tight sweaters that accentuated her curves.

Barely realizing it, she was constructing her persona—a contradictory mix of shyness and sensuality that made her irresistible. She bleached her hair lighter to look ever more like Jean Harlow, the idol of her childhood, who, contemplating herself in the mirror in the movie *Red-Headed Woman*, asks: "So guys prefer blondes, right?" The whole world would soon tell her that this, in fact, was the case.

A still of a scene in the 1952 movie Don't Bother to Knock.

The Scent of a Woman

*"What do I wear to bed?
Two drops of Chanel N°5."*

Seduction and marketing are intertwined in the sexy story linking Marilyn Monroe to the House of Chanel's most famous perfume. In 1952, a nosy journalist from Life *magazine asked the actress what she wore to bed. Without losing a beat, Marilyn replied with a mischievous smile: "Just a few drops of Chanel N°5." With these words, Hollywood's most famous diva forever bound her name to that of the fragrance, elevating it to a symbol of seduction and desire. Sales skyrocketed, transforming what had already been the world's most famous perfume into a legend. The bond between the American star and the French* eau de parfum *became indissoluble and was confirmed anew by a photo shoot taken on March 24, 1955. In it, Marilyn—more beautiful than ever—is captured posing with a perfume bottle in a room at the Ambassador Hotel in New York City, shortly before leaving for the Morosco Theatre on Broadway to attend the premiere of Tennessee Williams's* Cat on a Hot Tin Roof. *From that moment on, "the perfume by a woman that smells like a woman," as Coco Chanel described it in the early 1920s, became a piece of Marilyn, an essence bearing the memory of that eternal myth for the world at large.*

Gentlemen Prefer Blondes

Over the course of her merely sixteen-year-long movie career, Marilyn won the hearts of viewers with box office hits like Niagara, Some Like It Hot, *and* How to Marry a Millionaire. *Much of this was thanks to her talent, though also to her legendary fashion looks—like the pink gown she wore when singing "Diamonds Are a Girl's Best Friend" and her iconic "subway dress" in* The Seven Year Itch.

In 1951, Marilyn attended the Oscars award ceremony. Although she never received one, on that evening she had been invited to present the Oscar for best soundtrack. She came onstage in a black tulle dress with a plunging neckline that had been used by Valentina Cortese in a movie and borrowed from the Fox wardrobe collection.

Such fabulous stage outfits contributed enormously to her rise to stardom, which she planned with meticulous care. Her character was taking shape thanks to a wardrobe painted on her curves, her platinum hair-do, and a mole positioned in exactly the right place—plus a seductive manner of walking that made her unforgettable as the unfaithful wife in *Niagara*, a film noir set in the shadow of the famous waterfall. In it, Marilyn wiggled sensually in her heels in what is perhaps the longest walk in cinema history. Her signature sexy sway made her the only actress capable of making a memorable entrance while turning her back on the camera. Likewise contributing to the movie's fame was the scene in which she, attired in a tight, shocking-pink dress, provocatively whispers the words to the song "Kiss" as the vinyl hums on the turntable. Dazzling in her Technicolor debut as the evil Rose Loomis, she gave women a new weapon of seduction: ruby-colored lips with a satin finish that nobody but her could have made as iconic.

Marilyn in an elegant black tulle dress that she wore to the 1951 Oscars. Although she was asked to present the award for best soundtrack, she never enjoyed the honor of receiving the prize for herself.

On the top, the poster for Niagara *(1953).*

On the left and the following page, Marilyn captured on set. Directed by Henry Hathaway, the movie, in which she played the role of an unfaithful wife, launched her career.

"She had a luminous quality—a combination of wistfulness, radiance, yearning to set her apart."

(Lee Strasberg)

The film helped nail down Marilyn's career, catapulting her into Hollywood's hall of fame. Not yet twenty-seven, she had already appeared in as many movies, usually in the role of a ditzy blonde. The public identified her totally with the characters whom she played, placing her in a trap from which she would never be able to escape. Marilyn had become perfectly aware of this by the final weeks of 1952, during the filming of *Gentlemen Prefer Blondes*, a movie based on one of the most successful musicals of the time. In it, she played yet another beautiful but shallow woman, or at least so it seemed. She got her revenge by adding a line to the script—a fragment of a dialogue that conveyed her response to the sexual discrimination rampant in the 1950s and shed light on how things actually stood. "I become smart when it's to my advantage to do so, even if most men don't like it." Yet, the general public would remember Marilyn above all for the scene in which she sings "Diamonds Are a Girl's Best Friend," surrounded by a squad of men in black suits and projecting from the bright red backdrop in her pink evening gown. Having superbly paired her garment with gloves of the same hue, she became the mascot of the decade. The outfit dazzled with its cascades of diamonds: fake for the shoot but real for the publicity shots, during which Marilyn flaunted the famous Moon of Baroda. Her shapely body delighted costume designers, among them William Travilla, who dressed her for the movie and enjoyed a brief flirtation with her. "I have dressed so many women in my life, but never one like her," he recalled.

On the left, with Jane Russell on the set of Gentlemen Prefer Blondes.

On the top, the poster for the film, which was released in 1953.

On the left, Marilyn posing in the iconic pink dress she wore while singing "Diamonds Are a Girl's Best Friend" in one of the movie's most famous scenes.

On the top, a still from Gentlemen Prefer Blondes.

For this movie, he designed outfits that caused an uproar, such as the pleated gold lamé dress with a plunging neckline that could only be shown for several seconds because it was deemed too risqué by the censors. It was a sartorial masterpiece that accentuated the actress's figure to the maximum, so much so that Marilyn insisted on wearing it to the Photoplay awards ceremony. The producers tried to dissuade her, considering the gown too sexually provocative and ostentatious for real life. Ignoring them, she went ahead and did so, provoking an unprecedented outcry from the media. When making her entrance that evening in the golden dress that clung to her body like a second skin, she was greeted with thunderous applause. The next morning, she appeared on front pages everywhere. "Compared to her, every girl is insignificant," the newspapers declared. The scene in which Marilyn, departing for Europe on an ocean liner, bids farewell to her boyfriend as she sings "Bye-Bye Baby"—one of the great paeans to romantic love and immortalized here by the actress's sensual candor—likewise contributed to inscribing the movie in cinema history. Thanks to her excellent performance, she ended up on the cover of *Life* magazine alongside Jane Russell, the other principal member of the cast, whom Marilyn already knew as they had both attended the same school as girls.

Marilyn on the set of Gentlemen Prefer Blondes *in 1953.*

Ferragamo's Venus

Marilyn's sexy gait contributed to the immortality of her fame. It's said that she came up with a trick to make her walk more seductive: by having one of her heels cut by a quarter of an inch she swayed slightly with each step she took. Of course, like many other movie stars, from Audrey Hepburn to Greta Garbo, she preferred high-heeled but comfortable shoes, like those made by Salvatore Ferragamo, the best shoe manufacturer in the world. She owned dozens of pairs, all from the classic line but with a special heel—half wood, half steel—patented just for her. The Filetia and Viatica, detectable in sequences of the movie Some Like It Hot, *were her favorite styes. The ivory and beige versions were a wardrobe staple: on stage, she combined them with the extraordinary outfits designed for the movies, while in everyday life she wore them to round out her look of shirts and capri pants. Of all her shoes, the most famous are the red crystal-studded pumps with six-inch heels that she wore in the opening number of* Gentlemen Prefer Blondes *and that capture the essence of Hollywood glamour and high fashion to perfection. Salvatore Ferragamo was mesmerized by the actress, whom he considered a Venus on account of her tiny feet, a size 5 ½. To him, she embodied a particular type of woman: "Usually, a Venus possesses great beauty, glamour, and refinement, but beneath her glittering facade, she is often essentially a homebody who loves the simple things in life," Ferragamo wrote in his autobiography. "Because these two aspects stand in contradiction to each other, Venus is often misunderstood. People accuse her of too great a love for luxury and of frivolousness."*

"Give a girl the right pair of shoes and she can conquer the world."

"I leave to others the conviction of being the best, for myself I keep the certainty that in life you can always get better."

Notwithstanding the rumors of rivalry spread by the tabloids, the two became close friends. In the summer of 1953, they even knelt together on the sidewalk before Hollywood's Chinese Theatre while impressing their hands into the freshly poured concrete and leaving their mark on the Forecourt of the Stars. It was Marilyn's idea to stick a faux diamond in place of the dot over the "i" in her signature and thus refer to the song in the movie. The press spoke about nothing else for days, paying greater attention to this than to the coronation of Elizabeth II or Senator John F. Kennedy's engagement to Jacqueline Bouvier. The entire world looked on with admiration at this young woman with her irresistible, nearly insolent charm.

It was in that year that she first gained universal attention. Appearing on magazine covers around the world each day, she received 5,000 fan letters per week and took over the luxurious dressing room that had once belonged to Marlene Dietrich. She flew on private jets and was whisked around Hollywood in a helicopter, from which she would step out in tight, brightly colored dresses, much to the delight of photographers.

Marilyn Monroe and Jane Russell leaving their imprints in the fresh cement in front of the Chinese Theatre in Hollywood on June 26, 1953.

"They say that money can't buy happiness, but if I have to cry I'd rather do it in the back of a Rolls Royce than that of a subway car."

On the left, a poster for the 1953 movie How to Marry a Millionaire.

On the right, Marilyn and David Wayne in a scene from the movie.

Fame was gratifying, but not enough to make her happy. Marilyn knew that her talent as an actress didn't meet expectations. Her desire to get producers and directors to consider her for more intense and dramatic roles was consistently dashed thanks to her sinuous, provocative body that bound her to the role of sex bomb. The same thing happened again when she was handed the script for a sophisticated comedy titled *How to Marry a Millionaire* about three models who, determined to snag wealthy husbands, rent a penthouse in Manhattan. The two stars working alongside Marilyn—Betty Grable and Lauren Bacall—had fond memories of that joint venture, even if working with Marilyn wasn't easy. "She was often annoying, yet I couldn't help but like her. There was nothing mean or malicious about her, " said Lauren Bacall, who didn't show a trace of jealousy even after a photographer snapped a photo of Humphrey Bogart, her husband, mesmerized by Marilyn's cleavage at the movie's premier.

On set, as in real life, Marilyn could be as funny as she was exasperating. Sometimes, after doing her hair and makeup, for example, she would suddenly realize that she hadn't yet showered. So, everyone had to wait until she was done bathing and went through the entire process all over again. Initially punctual, she began annoying directors by showing up late—a habit that eventually became legendary. As she was terrified of not living up to expectations, some days it took all the patience in the world to convince her to go on set.

Support came less from directors and studio assistants than from hairdressers and makeup artists, like Gladys Whitten, whom Marilyn affectionately called Gladness. Feeling at ease with them, she showered them with gifts and affectionate dedications, such as the one on a photograph "to Gladys, because she's the one who makes me look like this. I love you."

In the movie, the camera captured the sweet naiveté of Pola, the character played by Marilyn, a young woman lacking in confidence, who, just like her, was desperate for affection. The actress's insecurity made her hyper-sensitive to criticism; if a director asked her to repeat a scene she might cry inconsolably for hours. She often forgot her lines, and her actions were terribly confusing: she would answer the phone before it rang or drink her coffee before filling the cup.

On the top, Marilyn on the set of How to Marry a Millionaire*, directed by Jean Negulesco.*
On the right, posing on set with actresses Lauren Bacall and Betty Grable.

Yet, despite all this, director Jean Negulesco ended up adoring her. "We had no idea whether she had acted well or badly. But once we put the film together, we realized that only one person on that screen was a great actress: Marilyn." On the night of the premiere, she entered the theater to the cheers of an adoring crowd, though she could not escape some spiteful comments from mudslingers. "This is the happiest night of my life," she told the press, before taking a swipe at her critics. "It would be wonderful to enjoy success without seeing envy in the eyes of those around us." Critics agreed, declaring the movie a success.

On the left, Marilyn in one of the promotional images used to launch How to Marry a Millionaire.

On the top, Marilyn along with Lauren Bacall and Humphrey Bogart at the movie's premiere at the Fox Wilshire Theatre in Beverly Hills on November 4, 1953.

In late summer 1953, Marilyn stepped off the train in Jasper, set among the splendor of the Rocky Mountains. It was against these never-ending vistas that *River of No Return* was to be filmed—a movie that would far exceed its anticipated budget and time allowance. The male lead was played by Robert Mitchum, whom Marilyn already knew, since, before becoming an actor, he had worked on an assembly line with Jim Dougherty, her first husband. In the movie, he assumed the role of a tough guy with a soft heart and Marilyn that of a seductive saloon singer. Once again she was asked to step into the shoes of the pretty blonde and sing several songs, feeding male fantasies with her simple-minded behavior and absurd anachronisms. To capture the Wild West culture of the nineteenth century, she was required to wear tight jeans, clingy shirts, fishnet stockings, and a pair of red heels. Letting tenderness prevail over eroticism in the final scene, Marilyn abandons her man on the street while performing the song from which the movie derived its name.

Marilyn's increasing apprehension regarding her acting skills was compounded by the physical demands of the set amid the mountains and Technicolor panoramas. The movie included breath-taking scenes, filmed along a rushing river. As the director did not want to use stuntmen, Marilyn ended up slipping from the raft and nearly drowning after her water-drenched boots dragged her down before hundreds of tourists watching the shoot from a distance. Although put to a hard test, she never complained. She knew her responsibilities well, and the crew adored her.

On the top, a photo of Marilyn with Robert Mitchum during the filming of River of No Return *in 1954.*

On the right, the actress on the set of the movie, which was directed by Otto Preminger.

Two photos of Marilyn taken during the shooting of River of No Return, *filmed against the spectacular scenery of the Rocky Mountains in the summer of 1953.*

Marilyn resting during the filming of River of No Return.

Marilyn and Donald O'Connor in a promotional shot for There's No Business Like Show Business *(1954).*

After marrying Joe DiMaggio in 1954, Marilyn decided to reduce her work commitments, but within a few months of their wedding it became clear that she had no intention to quit working. She thus agreed to star in *There's No Business Like Show Business*, a sparkling musical comedy with music by the composer Irving Berlin. In it, she danced and performed songs with titles alluding to her own romantic situation, such as "After You Get What You Want, You Don't Want It."

The actress wearing one of the sumptuous dresses designed by William Travilla for the movie and for which he earned an Oscar nomination for best costumes.

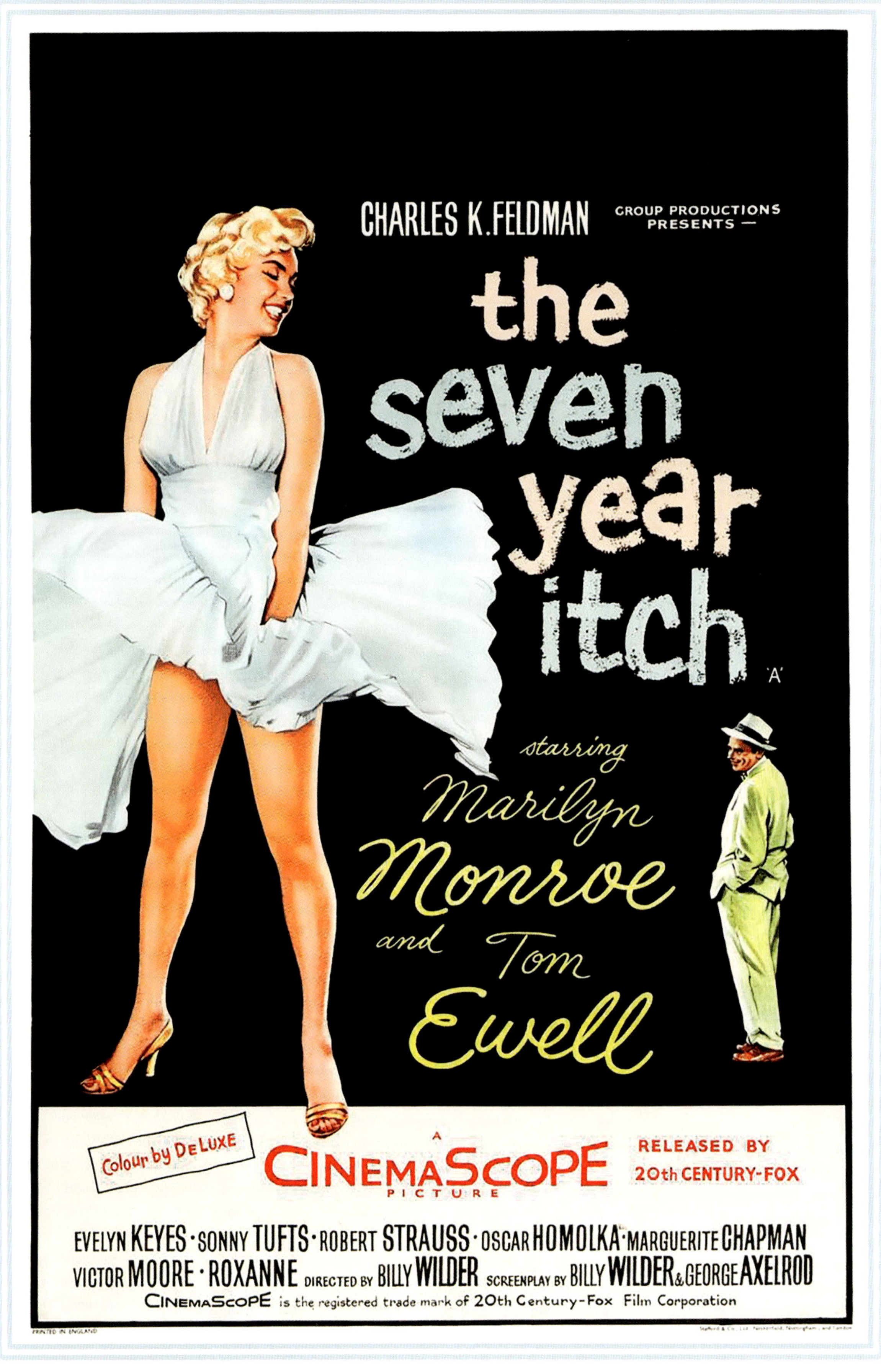
CHARLES K. FELDMAN
GROUP PRODUCTIONS PRESENTS —
the seven year itch
'A'
starring
Marilyn Monroe
and Tom Ewell
Colour by DE LUXE
A CINEMASCOPE PICTURE
RELEASED BY 20th CENTURY-FOX
EVELYN KEYES · SONNY TUFTS · ROBERT STRAUSS · OSCAR HOMOLKA · MARGUERITE CHAPMAN
VICTOR MOORE · ROXANNE DIRECTED BY BILLY WILDER SCREENPLAY BY BILLY WILDER & GEORGE AXELROD
CINEMASCOPE is the registered trade mark of 20th Century-Fox Film Corporation

On the left, a poster for The Seven Year Itch, *directed by Billy Wilder.*

On the right, Marilyn and Tom Ewell in a scene from the film, released in 1955.

Immediately afterward, without taking a single day off, she flew to New York to work on a new movie, *The Seven Year Itch*, directed by Billy Wilder. The script was inspired by the play of the same name, which seemed to be modeled on Marilyn's life, beginning with the name of the main character, Rita Marlowe, who was played on the stage by the actress Vanessa Brown. In the play, the curtain rises on a vacuous and vapid starlet, recently divorced from a legendary but violent and possessive athlete. In addition, the script makes constant reference to the entourage of agents, photographers, and directors with whom Marilyn consorted in real life. In the movie, as opposed to the stage version of the comedy, however, the female lead's virtue remains intact so as to escape the cuts demanded by relentless movie censors. Assuming the guise of an irresistible temptress, Marilyn ignites the fantasies of the leading male character, an employee who, having sent his wife and son on vacation, gets the "seven-year itch" for the blonde boarder upstairs. Alternating between provocative and subtle, Marilyn is able to play seductively with the audience, as in the scene where she appears naked while leaning from the balcony to inform her neighbor that she keeps her underwear in the fridge or dips French fries in champagne. These were remarkable scenes for the 1950s—at least as remarkable as the white dress that flew up in the movie's most iconic scene, which transformed Marilyn into a legend.

Two photos of Marilyn taken on set during the filming of The Seven Year Itch *in September 1954.*

Marilyn
NAME Monroe
DATE
9-13-54
The girl.
CHAR.
WRD. NO.
PIC. NO.
734
MKP. NO.
HDR. NO.
TAG

A party was thrown at the Romanoff—adorned for the occasion with a huge portrait of the actress—to celebrate the end of the film's shooting. Marilyn made her grand entrance in a red dress with a white fur stole, which she wore over her bare shoulders. Many had come that evening to shower her with praise: Hollywood producers Sam Goldwin and Jack Warner as well as actors such as Humphrey Bogart, Lauren Bacall, Gary Cooper, and Doris Day—even the legendary screen figure whom she had idolized as a child due to his resemblance to the father she had never known: Clark Gable. While dancing with him, she revealed that as a little girl she had believed he was her true father. Laughing over this, they promised each other to work on a movie together soon. Over the course of the evening, a photograph of Marilyn was passed from table to table and signed by each guest. The cinema elite had finally accepted her, and that evening, honored by all those stars, she felt at home for the first time.

On the left, the famous photograph of Marilyn in the fluttering white dress, designed by William Travilla for The Seven Year Itch.

On the top, the set-up in New York on the night of September 15, 1954, when the iconic image of the star was taken.

A Seductive Gust

It was chilly in New York that night in September. By midnight, a crowd of over two thousand people had gathered behind a barrier before the Trans-Lux Theatre on Lexington Avenue to watch the filming of Billy Wilder's newest movie, The Seven Year Itch. *Word had spread that there would be a sensational scene with Marilyn Monroe, and reporters had positioned themselves among the crowd that was chanting the diva's name under the vigilant eye of the police. Marilyn appeared in an ivory-colored dress with a halter neck and full pleated skirt, destined to become iconic. Custom-made by costume designer William Travilla, the dress embodied the delicate blend of innocence and seduction that the actress conveyed on screen. In what would become an unforgettable sequence in cinematic history, she is heard saying in a little-girl, Betty Boop voice: "Ooh, do you feel the breeze from the subway! Isn't it delicious?" apparently unaware that her dress was about to fly up. Escorted by the director, Marilyn positioned herself above the subway air ducts, after which the technicians turned on the giant fan mounted right beneath the grate. A gust of cool air shot up from beneath the actress's feet, simulating a passing train and making her dress fly up to her waist while revealing her legs and more. The scene was re-shot fourteen times and the filming took about three hours as photographers clicked their cameras non-stop. The result was a series of sensational photos that traveled around the world. Roy Craft, a media publicist who followed the film's launch, said that everyone at the scene that evening got so carried away that "the Russians could have invaded Manhattan and no one would have noticed."*

Actually, it was all a clever marketing ploy. The producers knew that the scene could have been conveniently filmed on a Hollywood set, but that would have failed to attract all that publicity. In any case, director Billy Wilder was dissatisfied with the sequence shot on the street that night and the one that appears in the movie was re-shot some time later in a studio. The costume used in the original ended up in actress Debbie Reynolds's private collection before being sold to an unknown buyer for an absolutely crazy sum—nearly five million dollars. And to think that when Travilla designed it, he described it as a "silly little dress." Even if it was a "silly little dress," once it was worn by Marilyn Monroe, it became a landmark of iconic cinematography.

"Hollywood's a place where they'll pay you a thousand dollars for a kiss, and fifty cents for your soul."

Yet despite her enormous success, Marilyn was dissatisfied. She sensed that she was being exploited by Twentieth Century-Fox, which had bound her to a financially unfavorable contract. Among the five stars in the world to earn more money than producers, she made far less than other actresses did. While colleagues like Liz Taylor collected millions in royalties, she was paid a paltry amount when it came to proceeds—even compared to Jane Russell, her co-star in *Gentlemen Prefer Blondes*, who earned ten times more. Though she lived like a star, she lacked money to maintain the lifestyle of one. Her only source of wealth lay in her fame. In addition, the roles she was assigned were all mired in the cliché of the ditzy blonde, and she was tired of waiting for something more challenging. She thus took on a battle that was to prove important, not only for her, but also for all the actresses who succeeded her. In January 1955, she called in reporters to announce something unexpected. "I'm fed up with sexy roles," she declared to those who had shown up to listen her and then proceeded to announce that she, along with her friend, the photographer Milton Greene, were founding a film company, Marilyn Monroe Productions.

After the silent movie star Mary Pickford, Marilyn was only the second woman in the history of cinema to take this step. By renouncing her contract with Fox, she was openly defying the all-powerful producers of Hollywood. Fed up with the routine sexual abuse and harassment in the studios, she publicly denounced the reality of Hollywood at a time when most actresses would never have dared challenge the world's most powerful movie industry. "You know that when a producer calls an actress into his office to discuss a script, that's not the only thing on his mind," she remarked. Decades before the #MeToo movement, she spoke openly about the sexism behind the big screen, launching widespread denunciation of the industry.

A photo of Marilyn taken by Larry Barbier in the mid-1950s.

To underscore her break with the studios, Marilyn decided to move to New York, intrigued by the rhythm of that delirious city. Dressed in a long coat, sunglasses, and a black wig, she took a flight from the Los Angeles airport under the pseudonym Zelda Zonk. Initially residing in a three-room suite on the twenty-seventh floor of the elegant Waldorf Astoria, she later moved into an apartment on Sutton Place and East 57th Street. She rode her bike through Central Park, shopped at Saks and Whelan's, and often escaped to Brooklyn for lunch at Nathan's, a hot dog stand in Coney Island. She devoured the *New York Times* and loved going to off-Broadway shows in Greenwich Village in the evening.

In addition, Marilyn began taking acting lessons from Lee Strasberg, the founder of the Actors Studio, the world-famous theater laboratory in New York that had launched the careers of Marlon Brando, Montgomery Clift, and James Dean. Strasberg's method was based on getting actors to draw on their personal experience to breathe life into the characters they played. For Marilyn, this was a tough challenge. Having spent years trying to forget her unhappy past, she was now asked to drag all those memories back to the surface. Digging into her tangled emotions, Strasberg untied the knot of her explosive power and took on the role of psychological guide and father figure that she had long sought.

Looking out from the balcony of the Ambassador Hotel, the actress admires the view of New York in March 1955. Photograph by Ed Feingersh.

In him, Marilyn found the master for whom she had been looking all her life and to whom she could entrust the formation of a new personality. "What was going on inside her did not correspond at all to her outward appearance. It was as though she herself was waiting for someone to press a button and, when that happened, the door would open up on a treasure trove of gold and jewels," Strasberg later recalled, intuiting an exceptional talent that would help her express herself in all her glory. Aware of her limitations, Marilyn would show up for class in a sweater and jeans, without makeup, choosing to sit in the darkest corner of the room. Diligent and attentive, she had one weakness: she was always late. Strasberg was inflexible on this point. When she confessed to him her inability to be punctual, he countered with a piercing retort: "Then make sure to arrive early."

Marilyn soon supplemented the classroom exercises with private sessions at Strasberg's home. She was warmly received by the family and often spent weekends and vacations with Lee's wife, Paula, and their two daughters. The one-time orphan had now found a new family willing to take her in. She repaid their hospitality by offering Lee a trip to the Soviet Union and participating in fund-raising events organized by the Actors Studio. Her very presence was enough to ensure donations. A year later, she reaped the benefits of that commitment. In her only theatrical endeavor, she performed a long scene from Eugene O'Neill's *Anna Christie* before an audience of colleagues and friends. Strasberg often spoke of her, praising her gifts. "I have worked with hundreds of actors and actresses, but only two have stood out from the rest: the first was Marlon Brando, the second, Marilyn Monroe." After years of having Natasha Lytess accompany her on set, she henceforth chose to have Paula, Strasberg's wife, at her side on all such occasions.

Protected by a pair of dark glasses, Marilyn enters the Elizabeth Arden Salon in New York in 1955.

OWN
CAL
AND
RAL
ST.

"Remember those who stuck around when you weren't doing well, because they're the ones you'll want at your side when everything is going well."

The two photo on these pages were taken at the subway stop at Grand Central Station in New York in March 1955.

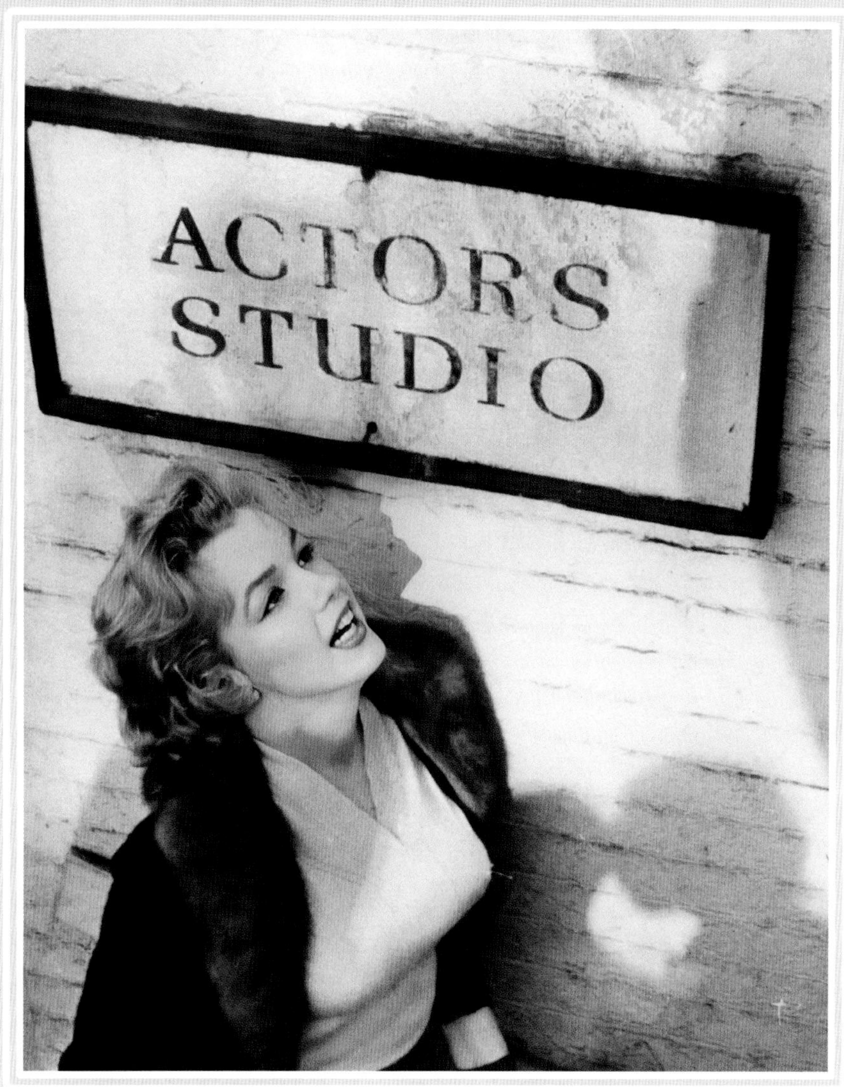

Empowered by her new experience, she was ready to return to Hollywood. When her flight from New York landed, she was greeted by a triumphal reception. A crowd of reporters were already there, waiting for her arrival, and it took two hours to disperse her fans and get her out of the airport. The shy, nearly childlike voice of her early career had disappeared, as she now gave lively interviews. Concerned about potential competition with Marilyn Monroe Productions,

Marilyn at the entrance to the Actors Studio in New York, where she attended Lee Strasberg's classes.

Fox renegotiated her contract, this time with highly favorable conditions. The new seven-year agreement guaranteed her adequate compensation, with the possibility of making one film per year with another movie studio. But above all, it granted her the right to refuse any movie she deemed unsuitable. The newspapers announced Marilyn's victory, calling it "one of the greatest triumphs ever attained by an actress."

The actress with Paula Strasberg, Lee Strasberg's wife, who served as her coach for a long time.

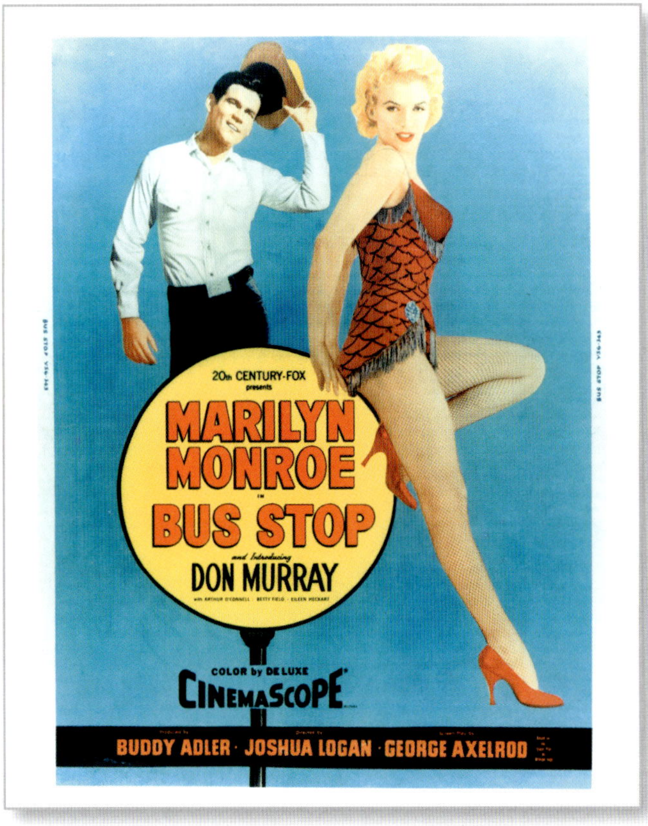

On the left, Marilyn and Don Murray on the 1956 poster for Bus Stop.

On the right, one of the images of the actress used for the movie's promotion.

Dressed in a sober black turtleneck, she seemed confident and poised when she announced that she was about to begin filming *Bus Stop*, based on a successful Broadway musical. Yet though the role of the singer Chérie seemed tailored to showcase Marilyn's talent, something inside her had snapped. The strain of shooting the movie in Phoenix, Arizona, in the scorching Sun Valley, brought on a series of anxiety attacks and a mental breakdown. Notwithstanding the difficulties, however, the film turned out to be excellent. Her intense and nuanced performance earned her amazing reviews even from some of the harshest critics. *The New York Times* called her "a genuine acting star, not simply the sex symbol she has been until now." In May 1956, *Time* magazine dedicated its cover to and ran an encouraging story on Marilyn, proclaiming her a successful actress with a glorious future. "Surprise! Here's an actress of great depth and talent."

For all that, she remained enigmatic to reporters who struggled to read her personality and shed light on her true story. They thus began sifting through her past, chasing after the real or fictitious clues that she herself had dropped about her unhappy childhood and many romantic relationships. While enjoying a trustful and understanding rapport with photographers, she was always wary of journalists. She prepared for interviews with care and demanded to know the questions in advance, terrified of the traps they might be concealing. Marilyn's insecurity was at odds with her image as a Hollywood star and man-eater, who, so soon after splitting up with Joe DiMaggio, was preparing to re-marry.

Bus
STOP

Marilyn with actor Don Murray on the set of Bus Stop. *Fresh from her experience at the Actors Studio, the actress fully immersed herself in the character of the singer Chérie, in what was to be one of her best performances.*

Two publicity photos shot on the set of Bus Stop. *Marilyn posing in one of the iconic outfits used in the movie: a green satin bodysuit with black sequins and gold fringe, paired with fishnet stockings and high heels. This was the look chosen for the scene in which she sings "That Old Black Magic."*

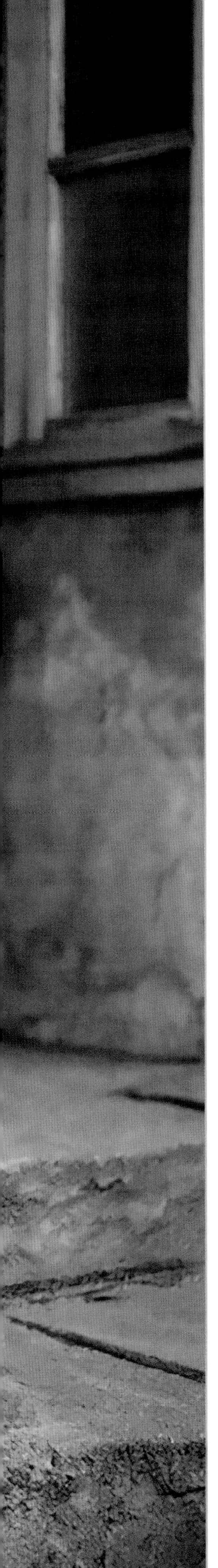

"We should all start
to live before we get too old.
Fear is stupid.
So are regrets."

Sexy and smiling, Marilyn poses for photographer Milton Greene on the set of Bus Stop.

"THE SLEEPING PRINCE"
LOP 301
001 01
DIRECTOR
LAURENCE OLIVIER
CAMERAMAN
JACK CARDIFF
INT:
NIGHT
DATE. 7/8./56

Several weeks after her wedding to playwright Arthur Miller, the two left for England, where Marilyn was to shoot *The Prince and the Showgirl* with Laurence Olivier, the British movie star, and likewise the work's director. This movie was, in fact, produced by Marilyn Monroe Productions. In this modern fairy tale, Marilyn played Elsie, the lead female character. Attractive and persuasive, she's a cynical and seductive showgirl who remains unimpressed by the luxurious life offered her by the Prince of Carpathia.

News of the couple's arrival in London appeared in all the papers even before shooting on the movie began. To avoid the crowds, Marilyn and Miller retired in absolute secrecy behind the gates of a villa in Windsor Park. Here they sought peace and quiet, and indulged in the pleasure of romantic bike rides during their idyll. The relationship between the actress and director Laurence Olivier proved far rockier, however. Fatigue and tension made the ambience on set impossible, while Marilyn's lateness became ever less pardonable.

On the left, Marilyn ready for action during the shooting of The Prince and the Showgirl. *Photo taken on set at Pinewood Studios at Iver, close to London on August 7, 1956.*

On the top, movie poster showing Marilyn in the arms of actor Laurence Olivier.

On the following pages, Marilyn photographed by Richard Avedon in 1957.

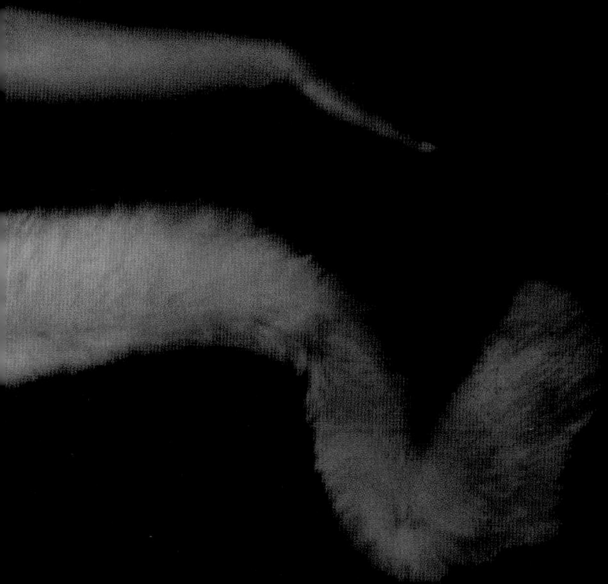

*“Miss Marilyn Monroe
calls to mind
the bouquet of
a fireworks display.”*

(Cecil Beaton)

An exquisite photo portrait of the actress taken by Richard Avedon in 1957 on the release of The Prince and the Showgirl.

On the left, hordes of reporters and photographers surround Marilyn during a press conference at the presentation of The Prince and the Showgirl *at the Savoy Hotel in London on June 16, 1956.*

On the top, the actress whispering something to Laurence Olivier, the film's male lead and director.

She kept people waiting all morning, forcing the crew to adapt to her impossible schedule. Busy on a new piece, Miller had to quit writing it in order to follow his wife on set to ensure that the film would get done. Marilyn was drinking and taking various pills to reduce stress—so much so that her psychoanalyst was summoned from New York to calm her down. At this point, Olivier grew more empathetic; he knew this kind of fragility well as it was the same suffered by his wife, Vivien Leigh, the unforgettable star of *Gone with the Wind*, whose moments of depression alternated with outbursts of violent anger. Despite all the problems, the movie enjoyed great success, and Marilyn proved both convincing and captivating. For the umpteenth time she was saved by the miracle that always occurred on screen.

Before leaving England, Marilyn met with Queen Elizabeth II during the course of an evening gala at London's Empire Theatre. The two queens—one of Great Britain, the other of Hollywood—were both thirty years old. Yet of the two, it was the actress, wearing a sparkling gold gown, who seemed truly regal. The sovereign, in turn, was dressed in a long and decisively more conservative outfit enhanced by the diamond and emerald Vladimir Tiara that had once belonged to the Archduchess Elena Vladimirovna. Notwithstanding the difference in their styles, both had covered their arms with long gloves, a distinct sign of elegance back in an earlier era. Shortly afterward, the actress's wax statue—in which looking like a goddess, she holds a glass of champagne in her hand—was unveiled at London's Madame Tussauds.

Marilyn meeting Queen Elizabeth II during a reception at the Empire Theatre in London on the evening of October 29, 1956.

SLH-L-7A

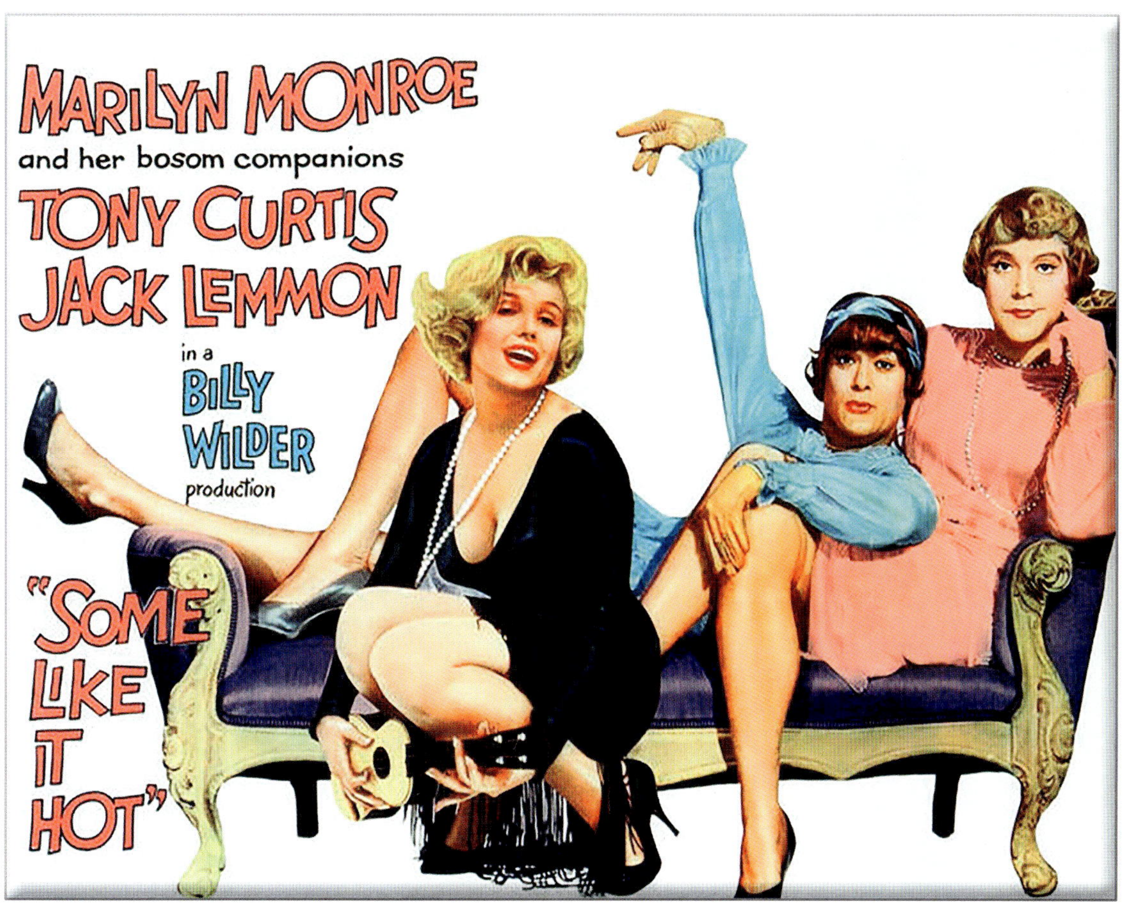

Afterward, Marilyn returned to Los Angeles to film *Some Like It Hot*, disembarking from the plane in a silk shirt unbuttoned to precisely the right point, a tight skirt, and her irresistible smile, which was immediately picked up by the hundreds of reporters crowding the tarmac. On the set, she once again joined forces with Billy Wilder, who had directed her in *The Seven Year Itch*. In this case, she once again played up to male fantasy as a seductive ukulele player who likes whiskey and millionaires and gets herself involved in a daring adventure with two men on the run, who, to escape a group of gangsters, disguise themselves as women. On set, her chronic lateness and inability to remember lines once again drove everyone to the brink of despair, despite the constant presence of Paula Strasberg at Marilyn's side. It took sixty takes to get her to say, "It's me, Sugar"; forced to reshoot the scene over and over, the director had to burn through miles of film. By now, Marilyn's fear of failure was bordering on neurosis.

On the left, Marilyn, Jack Lemmon, and Tony Curtis in a scene from Some Like It Hot *(1959), directed by Billy Wilder.*

On the top, the poster for the movie, which was set during Prohibition and the Jazz Age in Chicago in the 1920s.

A psychiatrist and doctor arrived on set to support what appeared to be another mental breakdown. What made working with her so difficult was above all her unpredictability: she would either collaborate or pose obstacles that prevented the completion of the day's shoot. As Billy Wilder recounted, "There were days when I wanted to strangle her, but then there were also wonderful days when we all knew that Marilyn was fantastic." Once again, she worked her spell. On film she managed to hide her anguish beneath a mask of dazzling beauty. Sheathed in a dress adorned with scandalously transparent beads, she seemed splendid and convincing in the movie, which again was a box office hit. To this day, it remains Marilyn's greatest commercial success, and the role in which she appears at the apex of her talent and beauty. So much so that she won the Golden Globe for best actress. It was in that year, too, that she received one of the very few international acknowledgments of her artistic career—the David di Donatello award, which the Italian actress Anna Magnani presented to her at the Italian Cultural Institute in New York City.

On the left, Marilyn with Jack Lemmon on the set of Some Like It Hot *in Coronado Beach, California.*

On the right, the actress during the shooting of the film. Beneath her overcoat is one of the splendid stage costumes designed by Orry-Kelly, who received an Oscar for his contribution to the film.

"Imperfection is beauty, madness is genius, and it's better to be absolutely ridiculous than absolutely boring."

Two promotional photos taken during the official launch of Some Like It Hot *in 1959. On the left, Marilyn joking with Jack Lemmon and Tony Curtis, who played the male leads in the movie.*

On the top, she holds the ukulele on which she performed as Sugar, the movie's female lead.

Several months later she was back on set. In 1960, Miller had written a story for *Esquire* magazine about cowboys on a ranch who caught and tamed wild colts. He thought it would make for an ideal screenplay for Marilyn—a gift of love that would promote the talent of his wife, who had long desired a dramatic role. Thus arose the idea for *The Misfits*, a movie directed by the great John Huston, with a cast of extraordinary actors that included Clark Gable and Montgomery Clift. Marilyn, meanwhile, was assigned the role of Roslyn, a brave heroine who struggles to save horses destined for slaughter. Yet behind Miller's dialogue lay the ruins of their marriage. Full of bitterness and resentment, the script drew lines from their arguments and the reproaches that he cast at her, rubbing her fragility in her face. Marilyn left for Nevada with a suitcase full of pills and no idea of the "hell" awaiting her. Without her usual armor of glitter and sequins, she had to muster up all her charm to transform herself once again into the dream woman. Simple and modern, she showed the world the allure of jeans—a pair of Levi's paired with a white shirt and Lee jacket with a corduroy-lined collar that artists like the great Paul Newman and Kirk Douglas had already turned into classics. Documenting the shoot were photographers from the Magum agency. Among these were distinguished figures like Elliott Erwitt and the renowned Henri Cartier-Bresson who saw in the fragile and beautiful actress, "a myth, what in France we call the *femme éternelle*."

Marilyn, surrounded by Frank Taylor, Montgomery Clift, Eli Wallach, Arthur Miller, John Huston, and Clark Gable, posing with the cast of The Misfits *for photographer Elliott Erwitt.*

E.T.
Gable
Marilyn M

Included within this group of talented reporters was Inge Morath, one of the few female photographers at Magnum. She turned out to be the ideal companion for Miller—and eventually his third wife after his marriage to Marilyn fell apart (the two, in fact, separated during the making of the movie). As tensions between Miller and Marilyn skyrocketed and rumors of divorce began spreading, Huston squandered some of the film's budget at a gambling casino. In her most demanding role ever, Marilyn gave it her all, working in scorching heat that often reached 104° in the shade. Consumed by anxiety, she took so many sleeping pills that in the morning she had to resort to stimulants simply to wake up. The results were devastating. Late in August, work on the movie suddenly came to a halt after Marilyn required hospitalization due to the blistering heat. Carried into the plane wrapped in wet sheets, she remained in the hospital for ten days. The star's condition soon became public knowledge. More bad news cast a pall on the completion of the shoot. Twelve days after the last take, Clark Gable dropped dead of a heart attack, leaving his wife pregnant with a child he would never know. For Marilyn, who had viewed the legendary actor as a father figure since childhood, this was yet another shock.

Marilyn and other leading cast members from The Misfits *on set in Nevada in October 1960.*

On the left, Marilyn and director John Huston in a Nevada desert rehearsing a scene from The Misfits.

On the top, the actress resting on set during a break.

On the top, Marilyn with husband Arthur Miller in Nevada during the filming of The Misfits *in 1960.*

On the right, the actress standing between Clark Gable and Montgomery Clift, the male leads in the movie, with two young extras behind them.

"Look at the stars.
They're all so bright,
but each of them must
be so lonely."

Marilyn on the set of The Misfits.

The actress with Clark Gable during the filming of the movie in fall 1960.

After depression and treatment forced her to take a long break, Marilyn began filming *Something's Got to Give*, the last movie stipulated by her contract with Twentieth Century-Fox, and one that she would never finish. A remake of a comedy of the 1930s, it featured a woman who had been presumed dead for years, but who nonetheless returns home the day her husband, played by Dean Martin, is set to remarry. The movie was directed by George Cukor, who had already worked with Marilyn on *Let's Make Love*. Not yet recovered from the deep depression into which she had fallen after the collapse of her marriage to Miller and woozy from all the narcotics she was consuming, she failed to show up on set, terrified at the idea of having to act. In her eyes, the gracious curves that had made her fortune had begun to sag, her svelte figure was disappearing beneath a few extra pounds, and her first wrinkles were leaving their mark on her splendid face. Her fear of aging was becoming obsessive. To get back in shape, she went on a strict diet, lost fifteen pounds, and reclaimed her sensational measurements of the time when she had posed nude for that calendar. The movie never appeared in theaters, but it went down in history for including one of the sexiest scenes ever shot—a midnight swim in a pool, to which Marilyn showed up in a flesh-colored bathing suit that was meant to be invisible, but proved far too visible. As a result, she disappeared into the dressing room and reemerged in a blue terrycloth bathrobe. Taking it off to get into the water, she appeared stark naked. Lawrence Schiller, a young photographer at the time, happened to be on the film set for a story commissioned by the magazine *Paris Match*. "You're already famous, now you're going to make me famous as well," he told the actress while shooting a series of photos of her from the edge of the pool. Thereupon she emerged from the water covered solely by a misty veil that barely concealed her dazzling splendor and, for a split second, exposed herself. The two of them chose the best shots, which appeared simultaneously on multiple magazine covers around the world and restored her status as a sex symbol, which she had been so fearful of losing.

It was also during the film's shooting that Marily escaped to New York to make her final, memorable public appearance. This time it was not in a movie, but in a performance at Madison Square Garden celebrating the forty-fifth birthday of the man in whom she was in love. "Happy Birthday, Mr. President," she whispered as the whole world listened.

A famous shot of Marilyn by Lawrence Schiller, who photographed her in a swimming pool on the set of her last movie, Something's Got to Give, *on May 23, 1962.*

*"I am good, but not an angel.
I do sin, but I am not the devil.
I am just a small girl
in a big world trying
to find someone to love."*

Marilyn singing "Happy Birthday" to U.S. president John F. Kennedy during a celebration held at Madison Square Garden in New York on the evening of May 19, 1962.

The Scandalous Nude Dress

As she prepared to walk onto the stage at Madison Square Garden, Marilyn was nervous. That evening she was to be the star at the U.S. president's birthday bash. It was May 19, 1962, and though John Fitzgerald Kennedy's forty-fifth birthday fell a few days later, that was the date chosen for a grand political event meant to raise funds for the Democratic Party. Many artists had hastened to perform in support of the cause, including Ella Fitzgerald, Henry Fonda, and Judy Garland. The idea of involving a star like Marilyn Monroe had not pleased the producers at Twentieth Century-Fox, who wanted her on set in Hollywood so that they could continue filming Something's Got to Give, *the movie in which the actress was starring at the time and destined to be the final, unfinished one of her career.*

In order to participate that evening, Marilyn had made up an excuse to flee Hollywood under wraps, and, while flying to New York, rehearsed over and over the song she would sing on stage. Several weeks earlier, she had contacted the French costume designer Jean Louis Berthault in great secrecy, asking him to sew her a dress that would leave everyone speechless. Jean Louis's most famous creation until that time had been the strapless satin gown worn by Rita Hayworth in the movie Gilda. *But from that night on, everyone would remember him for the nude dress, custom-designed for Marilyn but inspired by another legendary garment worn by Marlene Dietrich at a show in London. As close-fitting as a second skin, semi-transparent and floor-length, it was made of the thinnest of fabrics and studded with rhinestones, allowing Marilyn to sparkle under the spotlights. Beneath it, the actress wore nothing. She walked onto the stage in a dress that had been literally sewn on her, after downing many glasses of champagne to build up her courage. She sang a novel version of "Happy Birthday" in a voluptuous voice, very slowly and in an extremely seductive manner with a strong erotic charge. The audience, ecstatic, ogled her as if she were an apparition. "I might as well retire from politics, after such a sweetly sung Happy Birthday," Kennedy declared as the theater thundered with applause. All of America's high society was present in the hall, save one person: First Lady Jacqueline Kennedy. Aware of the relationship between her husband and the diva, she had decided to take a brief*

"Husbands are chiefly good lovers when they are betraying their wives."

vacation with her children despite the official nature of the occasion. Behind the scenes, lives and destinies crossed paths, as Maria Callas, the opera diva, complimented Marilyn on her performance.

At the end of the show, everyone wound up at a private reception at the home of entertainment lawyer Arthur B. Krim, where the only photograph ever to capture the diva together with the president was taken. Wearing her unique rhinestone dress, the actress can be seen standing before a bookcase and between the two Kennedy brothers. Shortly beforehand, she had presented the president with his birthday gift: a gold Rolex on which she had engraved the words: "To Jack, with love as always from Marilyn."

Scandalous, revolutionary, and absolutely timeless, the nude dress flaunted by the diva that night became a symbol of audacity and sophistication. Making history when it was sold at auction by Christie's in 1999, it was eventually purchased in 2016 by Ripley's Believe It or Not, a museum chain that exhibits curiosities and memorabilia. Among the many designers who have since reinterpreted it is Bob Mackie, who redesigned it for the pop singer Cher. In 2022, the dress was worn by Kim Kardashian at the Met Gala to evoke the eternal allure and sensuality of the most beloved diva of all time.

Loved by the Entire World

With success came many lovers. From Joe DiMaggio, who loved Marilyn until the end of his life, to Yves Montand and Arthur Miller, and from Frank Sinatra to the most powerful man in the world, John F. Kennedy, to whom she famously whispered, "Happy Birthday, Mister President."

Despite having the world at her feet, Marilyn never felt as desired as she would have liked to have been. Her insatiable hunger for affection was born of her traumatic beginnings, of a painful childhood that had left her insecure, demanding, and difficult to love. Yearning for a family, she needed someone to hold her in their arms. Not for sexual reasons, but simply to provide her with support. Perhaps this was what made her so enticing: beneath the glittering veneer of celebrity, she was nothing but a vulnerable child seeking protection from a host of men who, in their own way, tried to provide her with the love that she so terribly craved. Endlessly flirting, she had affairs with many and became the wife of three.

Marilyn rarely alluded to her first marriage. Celebrated when she was barely sixteen, it had served as her passport to independence, an alternative as good as any other for getting out of foster homes for good. Tall with thick brown hair and blue eyes, Jim Dougherty was the twenty-one-year-old son of a neighbor. Working night shifts as a mechanic at Lockheed Aircraft and driving a Ford coupé, he soon caught the eye of a very young Norma Jeane Mortenson, oblivious of what the future had in store for her. The wedding was set for June 1942 so that the bride could reach the legal marriageable age according to California law.

A sixteen-year-old Norma Jeane in bridal garb, with a veil over her still natural chestnut-colored hair.

Official photos of Norma Jeane and Jim Dougherty's wedding, celebrated on June 19, 1942, in Los Angeles.

Printed on the wedding invitations was the name Norma Jeane Baker, despite the fact that the bride's signature on the marriage certificate stated Norma Jeane Mortensen. Only members of Jim's family and several of the bride's schoolmates were present to honor the new couple. The wedding photos show her smiling and wearing a long, traditional gown with an immense veil covering her hair—still dark at the time—and a single piece of jewelry, a simple pearl necklace around her neck. After a brief honeymoon along a lake in Ventura County, Jim and Norma Jeane moved into a studio apartment in Sherman Oaks. Nonetheless, it soon became clear that she could give nothing but a half-hearted performance in the role of the happy bride. She hated to cook, so much so, that she would accidentally pour salt into her coffee, serve fish raw, and developed a fear of handling meat. Even the couple's intimate life disappointed her. "Of course, I was not well informed about sex. So, after a while, marriage left me indifferent," she later recalled. A year after their wedding, Dougherty joined the Merchant Marine and was stationed at Catalina Island, off the coast of Los Angeles, where he moved with his young wife. To stay in shape, Marilyn took weight-lifting lessons from a former Olympic champion, and thus impressed men in uniform who vied with each other to dance with her at the evening gatherings organized for young sailors. She seemed to find joy in that male world, where she was admired for her splendid figure and exquisite face. Things changed, however, after Dougherty was sent on a mission to the Pacific. "Had I not joined the Merchant Marine during World War II, she would still be Mrs. Dougherty today," he declared years later. The truth was, Jim wanted a family, Marilyn a career. Her movie debut marked the conclusion of their marriage in divorce as soon as Dougherty returned from the war, a mere four years since their nuptials.

"I have always been deeply terrified to really be someone's wife since I know from life one cannot love another, ever, really."

On the left, Norma Jeane and her husband, Jim Dougherty, on Catalina Island in 1945.

On the top, the couple posing for a photo during a dinner shortly after their wedding.

Free at age twenty to devote herself to her dream of becoming an actress, Marilyn sought not another husband, but someone willing to embrace her and offer her disinterested assistance. "I had no friends. I had teachers and people whom I could look up to with admiration, but no one on my level," she claimed with bitterness. At the root of her emotional loneliness lay her constant need for recognition. In as much as she genuinely wanted to love others, she was capable only of loving herself. A narcissist, she loved checking herself out in the mirror, admiring the face from which those glossy red lips projected, their sensuality underscored by a mole deliberately fabricated to make them stand out even more.

And yet men couldn't help but love her. Able to make them wait for hours without rousing their anger, she could manage several simultaneous relationships without provoking jealousy. "She made you feel as if you were the only one, even if you weren't," claimed the famous costume designer Billy Travilla, one of her many lovers. In the movie world she developed a special bond with Marlon Brando, the most famous actor to emerge from the Actors Studio. She had admired him since his appearance in *On the Waterfront* and admitted to the press that she found him captivating. "There are people one reacts to and others to whom one doesn't. I react to men. For example, I react to Marlon Brando." She never attained her goal of working alongside him, but they did enjoy a brief fling in 1955, as testified by a photo taken at a charity event in December of that year and in which they appear happy in each other's company. Although the flame subsided after several weeks, they remained friends for the rest of their lives. The writer Truman Capote, too, loved Marilyn, albeit platonically, and based the character of Holly Golightly in *Breakfast at Tiffany's* on her. "Marilyn has a presence, a brilliance, a sparkling intellect. Something so subtle that it could never appear on stage, but only be captured on camera. Like a hummingbird in flight," he noted. Marilyn's unabashed beauty was the exact opposite of Audrey Hepburn's reserved glamour, who, despite Capote's preference for Marilyn, won the lead role in the movie—destined to become a cinema classic—based on his most famous book. Rumors of a relationship with Prince Rainier of Monaco likewise got around. The idea originated with Aristotle Onassis, the Greek magnate and companion of Maria Callas who later married Jacqueline Kennedy. It was he who pointed out that the principality overlooking the French Riviera needed a movie star to break out of its torpor and regain its luster. He wasn't wrong, but the prince's choice fell on another American actress, Grace Kelly. Amused by the idea of proposing herself in Kelly's place, Marilyn admitted defeat and called the actress in order to congratulate her in her own way. "I'm glad you found a way out of this business," she told her.

On the left, the actress with her friend Marlon Brando.

On the top, Marilyn dancing with Truman Capote in New York.

On the left, Marilyn wielding a baseball bat for a public relations photo in 1952.

On the right, she appears smiling at dinner with baseball champ Joe DiMaggio.

Although for Marilyn the idea of another marriage still seemed far away, she soon changed her mind. On the evening she turned twenty-six, she was staying at the Bel Air Hotel, recovering from an appendectomy. Despite receiving a huge mound of gifts and telegrams, she dined alone that night while engaged in a long phone conversation with the famous athlete Joe DiMaggio. After making history with the New York Yankees, the champ had scored his final home run on a baseball field in 1951 but remained a star for the rest of his life. He appeared in coffee ads and sporadically popped up at golf courses and the San Francisco restaurant that bore his name. His love for Marilyn came like a thunderbolt, flaring up as quickly as the camera flashes of the reporters who immediately transformed it into a media event. They first met some months earlier, in the spring of 1952, thanks to a publicity photo in which Marilyn, wobbly in her high heels, clumsily swings a baseball bat.

Impressed, DiMaggio requested to meet with her, so they agreed on a dinner. A dozen years older than the actress, Joe was an innately elegant, robust fellow with an old-fashioned kind of gallantry. Marilyn had expected a garish, loud athlete, but instead found herself sitting before a silent boy. "He was different from the way I had imagined him," she later recalled. Of Italian origin, Joseph Paul DiMaggio was the eighth of nine children born to a Sicilian couple that had emigrated to the United States. Meant to follow his father's profession as a fisherman, he suffered from seasickness and preferred striking balls using a broken oar as his bat. He was not yet twenty when talent scouts on the lookout for potential baseball players discovered him. Two years later he was playing at New York's Yankee Stadium. Although a brief marriage to a movie star had made him the father of Joe Jr., at age thirty-seven the king of baseball was rich and single, seeking a new queen.

After that first dinner, the two met again on the set of *Monkey Business,* in which Marilyn was starring at the time, and posed together for a photograph. The image made its way around the world, transforming their encounter into a love story that monopolized the international press. The courtship lasted a long time as Marilyn, waiting for him to decide whether to make their relationship official, exacerbated Joe's jealousy with her more or less secret affairs with other men.

In the meantime, the public became convinced that Marilyn was the champ's girlfriend thanks in part to the hints she passed on to her journalist friends. The image of America's most beloved couple was based on their more or less true revelations to the media, such as the fact that Marilyn had learned how to cook spaghetti for her future Italian American husband. Rumors of an imminent wedding had been circulating for months when, on January 14, 1954, the couple presented themselves unannounced to a judge in San Francisco demanding that he join them in matrimony.

Once again, Marilyn demonstrated her extraordinarily intuitive understanding of public relations. While waiting patiently for the clerk to fill out the forms of the marriage license, she made several calls to reporters. Thus, what was supposed

On the left, Marilyn and Joe DiMaggio leaving San Francisco City Hall right after tying the knot on January 14, 1954.

Marilyn besieged by Japanese photographers on her arrival in Tokyo in early 1954.

to have been a secret wedding instantly became public knowledge. As they left the town hall, the newlyweds were met by a crowd as well as a handful of journalists who bombarded them with questions about how many children they were thinking of having. DiMaggio assured them that there would be at least one, while Marilyn claimed that she wanted six. "From now on my most important career will be my marriage," declared the actress, looking lovelier than ever. Wearing a chocolate-colored suit with an ermine collar adorned with a brooch, she carried a small bouquet of orchids that granted a mere glimpse of the precious diamond ring that her husband had just slipped on her finger. To escape the crowd, they drove away in a blue Cadillac to the modest Clifton Hotel, where they remained locked in their room for an entire day before disappearing for two weeks. Finding refuge in the total solitude of the mountains near Palm Springs, they really

Marilyn and Joe DiMaggio during their honeymoon in Japan.

got to know each other during long walks and over billiards. As a celebration of their love, Marilyn gave her husband a gold medallion for his watch chain engraved with a phrase from Antoine de Saint-Exupéry's *Little Prince*: "True love is visible not to the eyes, but to the heart, because eyes can be deceived."

The honeymoon continued in Japan, where DiMaggio was scheduled to do a promotional tour for baseball. The crowds of admirers, however, were all for his famous wife. Besieged by Marilyn fans, the couple had to leave the Tokyo airport through a side exit after agreeing to attend a press conference with a hundred journalists, who flooded Marilyn with inappropriate questions about the way in which she walked and what she preferred to wear to bed at night. She kept a straight face even when asked whether she wore underwear, to which she acerbically replied: "Tomorrow I'll buy a kimono."

Distrustful and sullen, DiMaggio shunned publicity, while Marilyn longed for it. Though they did love each other, Marilyn could not help but enjoy the feeling of being every man's fantasy. So, while DiMaggio was busy with games and meetings with Japanese sportscasters, she accepted the U.S. Army's invitation to take a short trip to Korea and perform before American troops. Heedless of the freezing temperature, she appeared on an improvised stage wearing a sparkling sequined purple evening gown that left little to the imagination and a pair of gold high-heeled sandals, thus transforming herself into the angel of pleasure of every man's desire. Pushing aside a rough hemp curtain, she made her entrance before an audience of several thousand soldiers, who welcomed her with a deafening roar, applauding enthusiastically as she sang "Bye Bye Baby" and "Do It Again." "Never before had I felt like a star. For the first time in my life, I wasn't afraid of anything, I simply felt

On the left, Marilyn performing for American troops stationed in Korea in February 1954.

On the right, the actress in a U.S. Army helicopter.

happy. It was marvelous," she admitted, gratified by the unconditional love of the soldiers, to whom she had felt obliged to give her all. As she boarded the plane that would bring her back to her husband, she held back her tears as she paid farewell to the men waving their caps and shouting "Hurrah!" Joe seemed unmoved by her experience even as she excitedly recounted the thrill she had felt while performing before ten thousand people who stood up to applaud her. Dismissive, he responded by telling her that when he had played baseball, his audience had normally amounted to seventy thousand. In private, he differed from the quiet hero contrived by the American imagination. Moreover, the realization that Marilyn would never leave the movies opened up a chasm between them. "He wanted that I be the former actress, just as he was the amazing former player," Marilyn remarked, already tired of playing the role of the good wife.

Thus the shadow of divorce hung over them even before their honeymoon came to an end. Strong physical attraction was not enough to compensate for everything that kept them asunder, and the marriage, which began with contention, lasted under nine months. Indeed, they had little in common. While Marilyn liked going to the theater, seeing friends, and discussing books or movies, such things were of little interest to Joe. He preferred spending time in front of a TV, which made her feel like the neglected child she had once been. Their relationship soon turned into a tug-of-war between two increasingly detached characters. The more attention she attracted, the more possessive he became. In an attempt to catch her with one of her alleged lovers, he hired a detective. Along with his friend Frank Sinatra, the three broke into the wrong apartment and terrified an elderly tenant—an incident remarkably like one in a brilliant Hollywood comedy in which Marilyn had starred.

The crisis culminated during the filming of the famous scene in *The Seven Year Itch*—the one that was to make Marilyn iconic. Standing in the crowd gathered to watch the shooting was DiMaggio—shocked to see his wife smiling on the subway grate as the roar of the crowd rose and fell in sync with her skirt. That night, the crew staying in the rooms next to the actress's suite at the St. Regis Hotel clearly heard Joe shouting, while the following day wardrobe workers on the set noticed bruises on Marilyn's arms and back. "The first time a man hits you, you get angry. The second time he does it, you'd be crazy to stay," she confided to her hairdresser. Two weeks later, she filed for divorce. Hordes of reporters flocked to the couple's home on Palm Drive, while tour companies rerouted their itineraries so that their buses could pass in front of the house. Alone and in grief, DiMaggio never fully reconciled himself to the situation and went down in history as the lonely giant who remained hopelessly in love with the star for the rest of his life.

Marilyn and Joe DiMaggio in 1955.

"I love you so much that what you are is reflected back on me."

(Arthur Miller)

After the divorce, Marilyn took charge of her life. By now, at age twenty-eight, everything she did became a public event. Obsessed with her image, she wanted to cast aside her glamorous mask and reveal the complex woman and talented artist she felt that she was underneath. That was the year she discovered acting and other arts, including poetry, to which she had never had the time to devote herself. It was also the year in which she first felt truly in love; having caught the greatest American playwright of that time in her hook, all she had to do was pull on the line to make him hers.

Marilyn was introduced to Arthur Miller by director Elia Kazan at a party. "It was like hitting a tree. You know, like a cold drink when you have a fever," she later said, recalling that initial encounter. She instantly decided that she wanted that man, and quickly got him. Tall, serious, with dark hair and a scruffy appearance, Miller was the son of an industrialist ruined by the Great Depression. Growing up, he had done a thousand odd jobs to pay for his studies at the University of Michigan, from which he launched a career as a writer.

A photo portrait of the American playwright, novelist, journalist, and screenwriter Arthur Miller (1915–2005).

When he met Marilyn, he, along with Tennessee Williams, were the most famous playwrights in America. Married to his college girlfriend, Miller had two children. He was living in Brooklyn, where he had grown up, while Marilyn was still working in Hollywood. They met again after she moved to New York in 1955. Miller was about to turn forty; Marilyn was ten years his junior. "I had no idea she was coming to town until I read about it in the papers," Miller claimed. He well remembered that young woman, by whose sensitivity and extraordinary beauty he had been struck. "The sight of her was something akin to pain; I knew I had to run away or entrust myself to a fate beyond all certainty," he wrote. One meeting was enough to ignite the spark, though they managed to date in secret for nearly a year without the press's knowledge. They took bike rides together on the deserted streets of Coney Island and sought refuge in restaurants on the city's outskirts, sitting at secluded tables where no one recognized them. Marilyn kept a photograph of Miller by her bed and shared her secret only with a small circle of trustworthy friends.

In 1956, Miller announced that he and his wife had filed for divorce. While waiting for the verdict, he and Marilyn spoke on the phone every day, using nicknames to avoid rousing suspicion. Inspired by Vina Delmar's novel *About Mrs. Leslie*—the story of a married man and a nightclub singer who spend several weeks per year living as husband and wife—they referred to each other as Mr. and Mrs. Leslie.

Soon, they would no longer need to resort to such subterfuge. In June 1956, they announced their wedding, which was to be one of the most sensational ones of the era. To avoid the mass hysteria of the photographers milling around their homes, they held a hasty civil ceremony away from the cameras. Just as had happened three years earlier when Marilyn had wed Joe DiMaggio, the couple interrupted the judge at dinner to demand that he immediately perform the wedding. Dressed in a simple skirt and sweater, Marilyn filled out the marriage license papers, declaring her father's name to be Edward Mortenson and admitting her actual age was thirty. Miller, forty-one, had on a suit without a tie and borrowed a ring to put on his bride's finger.

Marilyn and Arthur Miller biking in the English park at Windsor on August 13, 1956.

Not a single photo captured that quick, less than five-minute-long ceremony. Two days later, they celebrated their union once again, this time with a romantic reception at the home of Miller's Hollywood agent, Kay Brown. Since Miller's parents were observant Jews, Marilyn decided that she wanted to get married according to Jewish custom. This time she wore a real wedding dress in cream-colored satin with delicately puffed sleeves and ribbons running beneath her breasts, covering her face with a short taffeta veil and her hands with a pair of white gloves. Around twenty guests toasted the couple with champagne and lobster at a garden luncheon. The ceremony was officiated by Marilyn's acting coach, Lee Strasberg: "This is the first time I've really fallen in love," she told Miller as he gave her a ring engraved with the phrase "From A. to M. June 1956. Forever."

In actual fact, the union lasted four years, despite the effort both put into succeeding at a relationship in which they had placed all their hope. In the beginning, Miller was utterly bewitched. As for Marilyn, it was the longest relationship of her life, and she committed herself to it with all her might. "Film is my business, but Arthur is my life," she explained to the press when she announced that she now wanted to devote herself to marriage. For the next two years she appeared in no movies. After a brief honeymoon in Jamaica, the two settled in New York, in an apartment on 57th Street that Marilyn redid with the help of interior designer John Moore. The house was decorated entirely in white and included the grand piano that Marilyn had had as a child and that she had found after a long search and on which she

On the left, Marilyn and Miller at their wedding reception in 1956.

On the top, the couple surrounded by photographers in New York.

occasionally plunked a few notes of "Für Elise." She covered the walls with mirrors and lined the shelves with all the books that she would now finally have time to peruse. Her encounter with this learned, profound thinker made her want to read and study. She pestered him with questions about the meaning of words she didn't know and took a curious interest in everything. For the first time she felt as though she was in the right place, protected and loved as she had always desired. Little by little she also won over Miller's children, Jane and Robert. "I'm really proud of them because they come from broken homes. I'm sure I understand them,

and believe that I love them more than anybody else does," she said about the two kids, with whom she remained in contact even after the marriage ended. She had always loved spending time with children, after all, and even her own approach to life managed to retain the simplicity and naiveté of childhood.

All that was missing to complete Marilyn's joy was a child of her own. In the summer of 1957, a few weeks before her thirty-first birthday, she discovered she was pregnant. As it turned out, the pregnancy was ectopic, so the magic spell broke within two months, causing Marilyn to sink into depression. Consoling her, Miller suggested that she move for a while to a ranch in Connecticut, where she could fill the void caused by the lost chance at motherhood through contact with nature and animals. In that idyllic setting, Marilyn poured all her affection onto their pets. In addition to their basset hound Hugo, they had Cindy, an orphaned mongrel they had picked up along some road, as well as a birdhouse and two parakeets in their garden.

The star got her smile back once she returned to the set to film *Some Like It Hot*, one of her greatest hits. Paired with the satisfaction Marilyn derived from this assignment was the joy of discovering that she was pregnant again. But this time, too, she lost the baby. Meanwhile, her marriage had hit a crisis. Neither she nor Miller were happy; while she felt drained, Miller was suffering from writer's block.

On the top, Marilyn stopping for a hot dog and Coke during a ride with Arthur Miller and photographer friend Milton Greene.

On the right, smiling while posing with her husband.

On the left, Marilyn and Miller in July 1956.

On the right, a romantic embrace in the garden of the house where the couple was living together in Connecticut.

Having completed his most recent work three years prior, he was unable to write another comedy until after Marilyn's death. Following a year of boredom away from the set, Marilyn felt equally dissatisfied. She thus returned to Hollywood, giving a fatal shake to their teetering marriage.

On the set of *Let's Make Love* she acted alongside the French actor Yves Montand, who played a wealthy businessman hiding his identity in order to seduce an actress, played by Marilyn. The male lead had been turned down by Gregory Peck, who did not want to deal with the nervous breakdowns for which Marilyn had by now become sadly notorious in the business. Cary Grant and Rock Hudson turned the role down for the same reason. The choice therefore fell on the captivating French actor. "After my husband, and along with Marlon Brando, Yves is the most attractive man I've ever met," Marilyn declared to the press. During the movie shoot that statement proved truer than anyone expected. Initially, things seemed to be going well; Miller was a friend of Montand's, who had settled in the Beverly Hills Hotel with his wife, the actress Simone Signoret. Marilyn and her husband had taken the bungalow next to theirs, and in the evening, the four of them would often meet for dinner. On the set during the day, however, the line between fiction and reality grew thinner and thinner.

"Love is our only form of immortality. Without love, what meaning is there in life?"

On the top, Marilyn and Arthur Miller with their basset hound Hugo.

On the right, the happy couple several months after their wedding in the summer of 1956.

Two shots of the actress with Yves Montand during the filming of Let's Make Love *(1960).*

More seductive than ever, Marilyn performed her role in black tights and a sweater, sliding down a pole while singing "My Heart Belongs to Daddy" with mischievous innocence. Because Signoret had to return to Europe for a work commitment, and Miller was coming and going from Los Angeles, Marilyn and Montand often found themselves alone in their adjacent bungalows. The idyll lasted until the end of the shoot, when Montand returned to Paris. Marilyn barraged the actor with phone calls, clinging to her hope that she could win him over after the press had caught them together in a limousine right before he left the United States. It was he who clarified the actual situation to reporters. "I've never met anyone like Marilyn Monroe, but she's still a child. I'm sorry, but no one in the world is going to ruin my marriage." Montand's bond with Signoret remained strong, so much so that the French actress observed with subtle irony: "If she's in love with my husband, that means she has good taste."

Miller's bond, by contrast, was coming undone. After Marilyn accidentally found her husband's diary, she discovered that he was having doubts about their love and felt embarrassed by some of her behavior. The end of the marriage occurred shortly thereafter, on the film set of *The Misfits*, which had been written by Miller and in which Marilyn was starring. At the end of the shoot, they returned to New York on two different planes and announced their separation. They also agreed that their dog Hugo would remain with Miller. As consolation, Marilyn received a white poodle from Frank Sinatra to whom she ironically gave the name Maf, inspired by the singer's well-known association with the mafia. Marilyn and Miller signed their divorce papers on January 20, 1961, the day that President Kennedy was inaugurated at the White House.

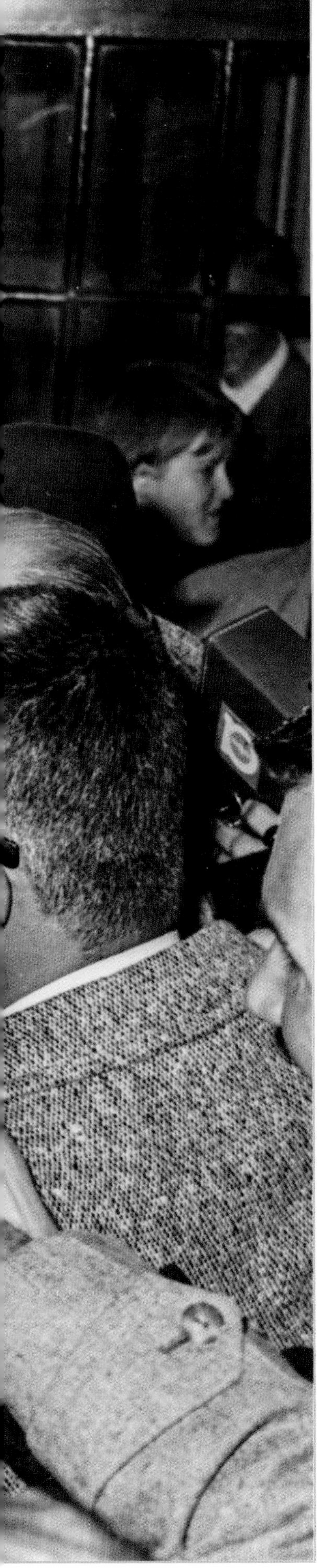

While the world celebrated the rise of this new young, optimistic politician, Marilyn's world was falling apart. She and Miller had chosen that day on purpose, hoping to avoid harassment by the media, though photographers chased her nonetheless, photographing her in her black outfit as she made her way through a crowd of reporters. She had fooled herself into believing that by being around a man like Miller, her image as a naive, sexy girl would disappear and give way to that of a woman who knew her worth and was committed to acting. Now thirty-five, she had never looked so gorgeous, but deep down she was beginning to die. Dressing in white most of the time, she bleached her hair even lighter as if to illuminate the darkness that was devouring her.

Surrounded by New York reporters, Marilyn announces the end of her marriage to Arthur Miller to the press in November 1960.

A Candle in the Wind

By the time Marilyn received her star on the Hollywood Walk of Fame in 1960, she was already a celebrity. Her premature and mysterious death two years later would shock the world and fuel her myth, transforming her into an eternal muse for visual artists and musicians, from Andy Warhol to Elton John.

Marilyn Monroe received her star on the Walk of Fame at 6774 Hollywood Boulevard in 1960. Although she had long since attained worldwide renown, her Christmas that year seemed like yet another of her sad memories of holidays spent alone. With Miller gone, she had found solace in alcohol, something in which she could drown her sorrow.

It was her ex-husband Joe DiMaggio, who, incapable of fully letting go of her, came to Marilyn's assistance on that occasion, arriving at her doorstep to brighten up her day. His unobtrusive but calm presence, however, was not enough to prevent Marilyn from descending into an abyss so deep that she was forced to recover in a psychiatric clinic. Arriving there bundled up in an enormous fur coat, she registered under a false name, terrified of what all this might lead to. "I'd always been afraid of going crazy, as my mother did, yet, when I ended up at a mental institution of this type, I realized that it was they who were crazy. I simply had lots of problems," she confided to her friend Susan Strasberg. The ghosts of her childhood all floated back to the surface, making her feel trapped. Once again, it was DiMaggio who realized that the place was not for her. Not a day passed that he did not go visit her, remaining at her side until her discharge. Upon returning home, Marilyn took time off to rest, refusing all scripts offered her. She spent entire days in bed, in a mental fog, dazed by drugs, surrendering herself to anyone who offered her a scrap of affection. "My bugbear is insecurity," she declared.

Marilyn absorbed in thought in New York, photographed by Ed Feingersh.

She had spent a lifetime searching among men for the father figure she had never had. This may also explain why she was always attracted to mature, powerful men, capable of making her feel protected. Writers, star athletes, actors, politicians, and producers, but also simple working-class men and great celebrities. Among them was Frank Sinatra. Marilyn attended his concerts, swaying to the rhythm of his music before the podium. The two even enjoyed a brief vacation on his yacht, accompanied by Dean Martin and his wife.

One evening when Sinatra came to pick her up at her home, he set a pair of splendid emerald earrings in her lobes just as she was completing her toilette. Although this seemed like the start of a new idyllic romance, it was simply the most recent of countless illusions. Several months later, the singer announced his engagement to another woman, and Marilyn returned the magnificent jewels to his press officer. Immediately afterward, Arthur Miller set the date of his wedding to his third wife, the photographer Inge Morath, who gave birth to a child seven months later.

On the top, Frank Sinatra on stage celebrating Dean Martin's birthday with Marilyn and Liz Taylor at the Sands in Las Vegas.

On the right, the actress dining with Sinatra.

"Never cry over a man
or you'll smudge your makeup.
And my mascara is worth more
than a stupid man."

It was also around this time that Marilyn got herself romantically involved with the most powerful man on Earth, John F. Kennedy. It is impossible to disentangle the truth from fiction in any reconstruction of the affair between the movie star and the U.S. president. Some sources insinuated that by this point in time they had already been lovers for years—ever since he'd been a young senator and she, Joe DiMaggio's wife. Some also claimed that Kennedy had fallen in love with the actress after admiring her legs on a poster while convalescing in a hospital. The two definitely met for the first time at a party in Beverly Hills held in 1951, but for a long time afterward their paths did not re-cross. The spark seems to have been ignited ten years later, after another encounter. The conquest of the two stars—one in politics, the other in cinema—was mutual. At the time, the name "Marilyn Monroe" was as powerful as that of Kennedy. They held their rendezvous in the presidential apartments at the Carlyle Hotel in New York or Santa Monica or at the country estate of Peter Lawford and his wife, Patricia, Kennedy's sister. Wearing large sunglasses and a man's coat, Marilyn would travel to these places under a pseudonym, her blonde hair hidden by a dark wig and scarf. In as much as the affair was a thrilling adventure for Marilyn, for Kennedy it was a form of mania that needed to be kept under cover so as not to expose him to public outrage or blackmail by the Mob. Marilyn, however, ran a far greater risk. As months passed, she came close to a breakdown. Even worse, when she drank too much, she became extremely talkative and prone to alluding to her liaison with the president to anyone nearby.

News that she had begun dating Bobby Kennedy—John's younger brother, who was attorney general at the time—had already leaked within the ranks of the president's entourage. When Bobby met Marilyn, he had already been married for a decade and just named "American Father of the Year." Although there's no evidence that the two did have an affair, they definitely became friends. The entire family was fascinated by the movie industry, and it was well known that its patriarch, Joseph Kennedy, had had an affair with a silent movie star, Gloria Swanson.

The risks the pair was running became ever more obvious after Hoover warned the family that the FBI was in possession of sensitive material on the two brothers, which the Mafia was planning to use as blackmail. The president and Bobby were sitting on a time bomb.

U.S. president John F. Kennedy and his brother Robert at a White House event.

Painfully aware of her fragility, Marilyn had been seeing psychiatrists for some time, a rampant practice among the affluent in California. Clearly, she needed some kind of help, but at that time it was not easy to distinguish professionals from self-proclaimed gurus who projected confidence and advertised their competence with the right rhetoric. While living in New York, Marilyn had spent several months working with Dr. Margaret Hohenberg, who pushed her to deal with her childhood traumas. This type of therapy threw the actress's life out of whack, without leading to any positive results. Two years later, when she again began searching for an analyst, she turned to Marianne Kris. For the next four years, she came to her office, which was located a short walk from Central Park and one also frequented later by Jacqueline Kennedy. She even found herself on the couch of Anna Freud, daughter of the famous Sigmund, who received her in the former London home of the founder of psychoanalysis when Marilyn was filming *The Prince and the Showgirl*. In 1960, she met Dr. Ralph Greenson, the last of an endless series of specialists to test their questionable psychoanalytical methods on the star. An internationally renowned figure, the author of important publications, and a professor of psychiatry at the University of California, he was known in Hollywood as "the analyst of the stars" since many of his patients, including Frank Sinatra and Vivien Leigh, were involved in the entertainment industry. Seeing Marilyn in his office nearly every day, he prescribed her massive doses of pills that, instead of helping her, made her sink deeper into hell.

One of the last photographs of Marilyn Monroe.

The phantom of the mad streak in her family haunted Marilyn during sleepless nights. She spent hours seeking solace over the phone, a lifelong habit that, in the early days of her career, had left her with multiple unpaid bills and a lawsuit by a phone company. "Do you know on whom I've always relied? Not strangers, not friends. The phone! It's my best friend," she used to say. She loved calling people at night when she couldn't sleep. In her home, she had two phones: a pink one that anyone could call, and a white one whose number was known only to a small circle of friends and acquaintances. Both had long cords that allowed her to move around the house while she was speaking. In the middle of the night, friends would receive frantic calls from her, begging them to throw something over their pajamas and come immediately to console her. Among these were women and men just as depressed as she was, who also had fallen into a downward spiral thanks to alcohol and drugs. It was thus that the formerly health-conscious young woman, who had once kept weights under her couch to stay in shape, crossed yet another threshold, that leading to Hollywood's world of addiction. Substance abuse had, in fact, been the scourge of the movie community since the 1920s.

To get actors through a film shoot, physicians often prescribed them barbiturates so that they could sleep, amphetamines so that they could stay awake, or narcotics so that they could relax. The rapid development of the pharmaceutical industry in the 1950s helped ensure the steady circulation of substances such as Benzedrine, which had the power to keep stars alert and slim by inducing a light form of euphoria and suppressing their appetite. Hollywood welcomed these new medications, which were often downed with alcohol and thus caused many deaths among depressed actors and producers threatened by bankruptcy. Movie studios viewed the pills as key to getting stars to perform their best, and there was no shortage of doctors willing to prescribe them.

Marilyn had been using drugs in immoderate quantities since the age of sixteen. She took amphetamines regularly in order to boost her energy. Indeed, her handbags were full of stimulants and relaxants, jumbled up with bottles of vitamins. In the final year of her life, she really slimmed down, losing nearly fifteen pounds and living on caviar, champagne, and hard-boiled eggs. She spent weeks without leaving her home or even combing her hair. This is why it took her hours to get ready and re-create herself as Marilyn Monroe whenever she needed to appear in public. Like a chameleon, she would make herself up to look more beautiful than ever. Even her voice returned to the soft, coddling tone that she used on screen, though if she drank too much, her reflexes slowed down and she stumbled over words and appeared distracted. After the champagne came the sleeping pills, a new sinister presence in her life. In an attempt to cure her chronic insomnia, she used massive amounts of drugs, going from one doctor to another to obtain even more. "When you're shooting a film you have to look good, and then you have to sleep. That's why I take sleeping pills," she said, justifying her habit.

By this point of her life, Marilyn was totally dependent on them; sleep had become practically impossible without the help of a few pills. She always kept a bottle of them on the nightstand next to her bed, downing them as late as 3:00 a.m., even when she knew she had to rise at six to go on set. On her way there, she took more in the car to fight off dizziness.

Overcome by exhaustion, Marilyn rests in an armchair during a reception in New York.

"I never wanted to be Marilyn—it just happened. Marilyn's like a veil I wear over Norma Jeane."

While rehearsing her lines over and over again in the dressing room, she always had a glass of champagne at hand, consumed as she was by the fear of her inadequacy and an anxiety that aggravated this insecurity. Clearly she was on the road to self-destruction.

On June 1, 1962, Marilyn turned thirty-six. That evening, she pitched a charity baseball game and received a champagne glass with her name engraved on it. "Now I'll know who I am when I drink," she said with a wistful smile. A few days later, she was fired by Fox, which sued her for her chronic lateness and repeated absences from the set of *Something's Got to Give*, leading to a sordid journalistic campaign to discredit her in the eyes of the public.

She resisted and spoke up at interviews, which the magazines couldn't wait to publish alongside the gorgeous photos with which they attracted thousands of readers. Smiling from the pages of *Life* and *Cosmopolitan*, she had lost none of her charm. At certain moments, it even seemed as though she had regained her old spark. Hyper excited, she frenetically made plans for the future. She contacted Gene Kelly to propose that the two of them work together on a musical set during the First World War; she spoke to a composer about her idea for a musical in which she would appear with Frank Sinatra. But above all, she wanted to play the lead in a movie about the star she had always adored: Jean Harlow. Marilyn also did one final photoshoot for Vogue—the famous "Last Sitting," which, catching her at one of her most intimate and vulnerable moments, revealed the woman behind the star, with all her disarming beauty and sweet vulnerability, covered with nothing but a translucent veil. Ben Stern, the photographer in this case, was mesmerized. "She was the light, the deity, the moon. The space and the dream, the mystery and the danger," he wrote twenty years later.

Thanks to that body of hers, Marilyn had made an exorbitant amount of money throughout her career, yet however high the sum, her financial situation was now suffering due to sloppy management and the uncontrollable costs of an army of doctors, secretaries, makeup artists, and lawyers, and gifts to various charities. Not long before, she had moved into the only home she had ever owned. "I didn't want a mansion like those of the stars in Beverly Hills, but a place for me and my friends," she said. She thus chose a modest house with white stucco walls and a red tile roof in the Brentwood neighborhood of Los Angeles in early 1962. The tiles at the entrance spelled out an inscription in Latin with a sad prophetic message: *Cursum perficio*, that is, "My journey ends here." Rumor has it that the house was full of listening devices that allowed the Mob—and possibly also the U.S. government—to listen to her phone conversations and intercept anything that took place in her bedroom. It was precisely in that room that she was found dead on August 5, 1962.

In the middle of the night, her psychiatrist Dr. Greenson was awakened by Marilyn's housekeeper, whose suspicions had been roused by the light in the actress's bedroom, the door of which was locked from the inside. Arriving at the house within a few minutes, Greenson broke the window to enter. Marilyn, lifeless, was lying amid messy sheets on her bed, her shoulders exposed. The photos taken by the police capture her thus, with her cheek resting on a pillow as if enjoying the peaceful slumber she had finally reached after a lifetime of insomniac nights. Was it truly a suicide?

As no definitive answer to this question has ever been given, it has led to multiple conjectures ranging from murder to an accidental overdose of barbiturates—a hypothesis no less tragic than the rest. Marilyn had tried to take her own life several times before this moment. Whenever she was overwhelmed by fatigue and depression, she stuffed herself with pills, seeking help in that silent act of desperation. Judging from her own account, she seems to have come close to dying in this way at least three times in the course of her short life. Toward the end of it she often spoke of suicide. "There's no other way out for me save death," she confided to friends when she drank too much.

The news immediately hit the world. Among the first to comment on the incident was Arthur Miller. "It had to happen. I didn't know where or when it would, but it was inevitable," he admitted to his friends. Joe DiMaggio, the other great love of her life, took charge of Marilyn's funeral. Inconsolable, he spent the night before the ceremony keeping vigil over the woman, whom he, more than anyone else, had loved. The next day, the notes of "Somewhere Over the Rainbow" resounded in the chapel during the service, to which only twenty-four people were invited. Among these were long-time friends such as the director of the Actors Studio, Lee Strasberg, who delivered the funeral oration, and members of Marilyn's dressing-room staff. Lying in a coffin lined with champagne-colored satin, Marilyn was garbed in a green dress designed by Emilio Pucci with a platinum-colored scarf covering her hair. A verse by the poet Elizabeth Barrett Browning was inscribed on her wreath: "And if God chooses, I shall but love thee better after death." She was laid to rest in a burial niche at Westwood Memorial Park.

Today the goddess lies behind a marble slab engraved with a simple inscription: "Marilyn Monroe 1926–1962." Once, while signing her will, Marilyn had joked that she would like her epitaph to read: "Marilyn Monroe, a blonde," then laughing, added: "37-23-36." Joe DiMaggio arranged to have two fresh roses placed before her grave three times per week for the next twenty years.

By her express volition, Marilyn left her mother a large trust fund that guaranteed her the assistance she needed until the time of her death, as well as a series of bequests for those people who had cared for her during her short life. All her personal effects, in turn, she left to Lee Strasberg, who had welcomed her as a student and offered her the warmth of a family. Clothing, fur coats, awards, books, letters, even underwear—all ended up in the Strasberg family's New York home. The boxes containing her poems and comments on life were stashed away haphazardly in trunks that were reopened only thirty-seven years later. Genuine treasures, crystallized—like the myth of Marilyn—in an eternal present, they were published in a volume entitled *Fragments*, reminding the world that before the icon, there had been Marilyn the woman.

Following her death, Marilyn's image transcended that of a movie star to become something far greater—a symbol of grace, allure, and vulnerability that has overcome the barriers of time and integrated itself into pop culture and the collective imagination. It was one that served as an inexhaustible source of inspiration for advertisers, musicians, and fashion designers, as well as a muse for hundreds of artists, from Willem de Kooning to Mimmo Rotella, Wolf Vostell to Andy Warhol, Richard Hamilton to Salvador Dalí, Robert Rauschenberg to Douglas Gordon, and Barbara Kruger to Mel Ramos, to name just a few of the more famous ones. In 1995, Gianni Versace created a collection inspired by the Marilyn look consisting of tight-fitting dresses and fabrics sparkling with rhinestones and crystals that celebrated her voluptuous beauty. With their sexy, feminine style, Dolce & Gabbana have also reinterpreted Marilyn with outfits and advertising campaigns that evoke her femininity. Great music stars have followed suit, starting with Madonna, who paid homage to the star who sang "Diamonds Are a Girl's Best Friend" in her "Material Girl" video, in which she replicated Marilyn's dress and movements in *Gentlemen Prefer Blondes*. Inspired by the actress's platinum hair, her sophisticated makeup, and red-hot lips, Gwen Stefani has adapted these to her own style, as has Lana Del Rey with her vintage appeal and melancholy-infused music. Lady Gaga, meanwhile, has paid tribute not only to Marilyn's look but also to her spirit in the retro and glamorous allure of her concerts. In the world of cinema, many actresses have tried to capture Marilyn's essence, bringing their version of the tormented life of Hollywood's most beloved star to the screen. In a moving performance, Michelle Williams played her in *My Week with Marilyn* (2011), a movie that shed light on both the weakness and beauty of the actress. More recently, Ana de Armas landed the role of Marilyn in *Blonde* (2022), a romanticized reinterpretation of her life that explores her psychological complexity and the challenges she faced. Today, Marilyn's legacy lives on not only in the great tributes paid her by the visual arts, fashion, and music, but also in the everyday manifestations of pop culture—photographs, posters, quotes from half a century ago that still fascinate and inspire millions of people. An echo of this resonates even in the music of Elton John.

Although the two never met, their souls seem to rub against each other in each note of "Candle in the Wind," a song that he dedicated to her in 1973. After Elton rewrote the work in tribute to Lady Diana, another icon of vulnerability, the piece became a universal anthem to all those whose lives had played out on the edge between love and despair. Whenever we hear the tune play, it's as though the wind were once again brushing past that candle that never goes out.

At the height of her splendor, the actress blowing a kiss to photographers and fans after landing in New York.

"Good-bye,
Norma Jeane,
though I never
knew you."

("Candle in the Wind,"
Elton John)

About the Author

A Milan-based journalist with a degree in art history, Chiara Pasqualetti Johnson covers travel, art, and lifestyle for top Italian magazines. She has edited books and series on the history of modern and contemporary art for Electa and Rizzoli, and authored a series of illustrated volumes on great female figures for White Star, including the bestseller *Coco Chanel: The Revolution of Style* (2020), which was translated into twelve languages, and *Chanel N°5: The Perfume of the Century*. These were followed by *Audrey. A Life, a Style* (2022) on Audrey Hepburn and *The Life and Style of Jacqueline Kennedy Onassis* (2023), both of which were translated into several languages. Her latest book, *Frida. Woman, Artist, Icon* (2024) has met with international acclaim after its successful reception in Mexico. In 2021, Forbes Italia included Pasqualetti Johnson among the 100 Wonder Women of the Year, an honor bestowed on successful women who exhibit leadership and creativity.

Bibliography

Badman, Keith. *Marilyn Monroe. The Final Years*. New York: Thomas Dunne Books, 2010. • Churchwell, Sarah. *The Many Lives of Marilyn Monroe*. London: Granta Books, 2004. • Dougherty, James. *To Norma Jeane, With Love, Jimmie*. Narrated by L.C. Van Savage. BeachHouse Books, 2000. • Franse, Astrid, Michelle Morgan, and Thomas Dunne. *Before Marilyn. The Blue Book Modeling Years*. New York: Thomas Dunne Books, 2015. • Guiles, Fred Lawrence. *Legend: The Life and Death of Marilyn Monroe*. New York: Stein & Day, 1984. • Leaming, Barbara. *Marilyn Monroe. A Biography*. New York: Crown, 1998. • Mailer, Norman. *Marilyn*. New York: Grosset & Dunlap, 1973. • Miracle, Berniece. *My Sister Marilyn*. London: Weidenfeld & Nicolson, 1994. • Monroe, Marilyn, with the help of Ben Hecht. *My Story*. New York: Stein & Day Publishers, 1974. • Monroe, Marilyn. *Fragments: Poems, Intimate Notes, Letters*. New York: Farrar, Straus and Giroux, 2010. • Newman, Terry. *Marilyn Monroe Style*. Woodbridge, Suffolk: Acc Art Books, 2024. • Nickens, Christopher, and George Zeno. *Marilyn in Fashion. The Enduring Influence of Marilyn Monroe*. Philadelphia: Running Press Book Pub., 2012. • Oates, Joyce Carol. *Blonde*. New York: Ecco Press, 2001. • Pasqualetti Johnson, Chiara. *Il profumo del secolo. Chanel N°5*. Novara: White Star, 2021. • Slatzer, Robert F. *The Life and Curious Death of Marilyn Monroe*. New York: Pinnacle House, 1974. • Spada, James. *Marilyn. Her Life in Pictures*. London: Sidgwick & Jackson, 1982. • Spoto, Donald. *Marilyn Monroe: The Biography*. New York: HarperCollins 1993. • Summers, Anthony. *Goddess*. New York: MacMillan, 1985. • Taraborrelli, J. Randy. *The Secret Life of Marilyn Monroe*. London: Sidgwick & Jackson, 2009. • Vitacco-Robles, Gary. *Icon. The Life, Times, and Films of Marilyn Monroe*. 2 vols. Orlando, FL: BearManor Media, 2015. • Wills, David. *Marilyn Monroe Metamorphosis*. It Books, 2011. • Winder, Elizabeth. *Marilyn in Manhattan. Her Year of Joy*. New York: Flatiron Books, 2017. • Wolfe, Donald H. *The Last Days of Marilyn Monroe*. New York: William Morrow, 1998.

Photo Credits

Page 2 PictureLux/The Hollywood Archive/Alamy Stock Photo
Page 5 Edward Roth/Alamy Stock Photo
Page 7 Michael Ochs Archives/Getty Images
Page 9 John Kobal Foundation/Getty Images
Page 10 Baron/Getty Images
Page 12 Baron/Getty Images
Page 15 Moviestore Collection Ltd/Alamy Stock Photo
Pages 16-17 Amadeo Torrero/Alamy Stock Photo
Pages 18-19 ScreenProd/Photononstop/Alamy Stock Photo
Page 21 JJs/Alamy Stock Photo
Page 22 Silver Screen Collection/Getty Images
Page 23 Historic Collection/Alamy Stock Photo
Page 24 Hulton Archive/Getty Images
Page 26 Silver Screen Collection/Getty Images
Page 27 Hulton Archive/Getty Images
Page 28 Silver Screen Collection/Getty Images
Page 31 Bill Waterson/Alamy Stock Photo
Page 32 Silver Screen Collection/Getty Images
Page 33 Silver Screen Collection/Getty Images
Page 34 Bill Waterson/Alamy Stock Photo
Page 35 John Rodgers/Getty Images
Page 37 ScreenProd/Photononstop/Alamy Stock Photo
Page 39 Diltz/Bridgeman Images
Pages 40-41 Donaldson Collection/Getty Images
Page 42 Donaldson Collection/Getty Images
Page 43 Donaldson Collection/Getty Images
Page 44 Earl Theisen Collection/Getty Images

Page 45 Pictorial Press Ltd/Alamy Stock Photo
Page 47 (top) Entertainment Pictures/Alamy Stock Photo
Page 47 (bottom) Album/Alamy Stock Photo
Page 48 Silver Screen Collection/Getty Images
Pages 48-49 George Rinhart/Getty Images
Page 50 Earl Theisen Collection/Getty Images
Page 51 Edward Roth/Alamy Stock Photo
Page 52 Philippe Halsman/Magnum Photos
Page 53 Bill Waterson/Alamy Stock Photo
Pages 54-55 Milton H. Greene/Morrison Hotel Gallery/AUGUST
Pages 56-57 Album/Alamy Stock Photo
Page 59 PictureLux/The Hollywood Archive/Alamy Stock Photo
Pages 60-61 Madison Lacy/Getty Images
Page 63 Bettmann/Getty Images
Page 64 Earl Theisen Collection/Getty Images
Page 65 Earl Theisen Collection/Getty Images
Page 66 Michael Ochs Archives/Getty Images
Page 67 Michael Ochs Archives/Getty Images
Page 68 Donaldson Collection/Getty Images
Page 70 20th Century Fox/Getty Images
Page 71 Michael Ochs Archives/Getty Images
Page 72 John Springer Collection/Getty Images
Page 73 Michael Ochs Archives/Getty Images
Pages 74-75 Hulton Archive/Getty Images
Page 77 Bettmann/Getty Images
Page 79 Keystone Features/Getty Images
Page 80 ARCHIVIO GBB/Alamy Stock Photo
Page 82 Pascal Le Segretain/Getty Images
Page 83 Michael Ochs Archives/Getty Images
Page 85 ScreenProd/Photononstop/Alamy Stock Photo
Page 86 Sunset Boulevard/Getty Images
Page 87 LMPC/Getty Images
Page 89 John Kobal Foundation/Getty Images
Page 90 Silver Screen Collection/Getty Images
Page 91 Entertainment Pictures/Alamy Stock Photo
Page 92 Allstar Picture Library Limited/Alamy Stock Photo
Page 93 ScreenProd/Photononstop/Alamy Stock Photo
Page 94 Donaldson Collection/Getty Images
Page 96 Cindy Ord/Getty Images
Page 97 Christie's Images/Bridgeman Images
Page 99 Hulton Archive/Getty Images
Page 100 LMPC/Getty Images
Page 101 20th Century Fox/Getty Images
Page 102 Sunset Boulevard/Getty Images
Page 103 Earl Theisen Collection/Getty Images
Page 104 ullstein bild/Getty Images
Page 105 Darlene Hammond/Getty Images
Page 106 Twentieth Century Fox Film/Diltz/Bridgeman Images
Page 107 Sunset Boulevard/Getty Images
Page 108 Twentieth Century Fox Film/Diltz/Bridgeman Images
Page 109 cineclassico/Alamy Stock Photo
Pages 110-111 Album/Alamy Stock Photo
Page 112 Michael Ochs Archives/Getty Images
Page 113 Michael Ochs Archives/Getty Images
Page 114 Photo 12/Alamy Stock Photo
Page 115 ScreenProd/Photononstop/Alamy Stock Photo
Page 116 cineclassico/Alamy Stock Photo
Page 117 cineclassico/Alamy Stock Photo
Page 118 MGPhoto76/Alamy Stock Photo
Page 119 Bettmann/Getty Images
Page 120 Business Wire/Getty Images
Page 121 Bettmann/Getty Images
Page 122 Hulton Archive/Stringer/Getty Images
Pages 124-125 Michael Ochs Archives/Getty Images
Pages 126-127 Michael Ochs Archives/Getty Images
Page 128 Michael Ochs Archives/Getty Images
Page 129 Michael Ochs Archives/Getty Images
Page 130 Bettmann/Getty Images
Page 131 Ernst Haas/Getty Images
Page 132 Archive Photos/Getty Images
Page 133 Archive Photos/Getty Images
Page 134 Archive Photos/Getty Images
Page 135 Archive Photos/Getty Images
Page 136 Donaldson Collection/Getty Images
Page 137 Allstar Picture Library Ltd/Alamy Stock Photo
Pages 138-139 Edward Roth/Alamy Stock Photo
Page 140 Donaldson Collection/Getty Images
Page 141 Archive Photos/Getty Images
Pages 142-143 Warner Bros Pictures/Diltz/Bridgeman Images
Pages 144-145 Warner Bros Pictures/Diltz/Bridgeman Images
Page 146 Express/Getty Images
Page 147 Central Press/Getty Images
Page 148 PictureLux/The Hollywood Archive/Alamy Stock Photo
Page 150 Michael Ochs Archives/Getty Images
Page 151 Entertainment Pictures/Alamy Stock Photo
Page 152 Donaldson Collection/Getty Images
Page 153 Donaldson Collection/Getty Images
Page 154 John Kobal Foundation/Getty Images
Page 155 Hulton Archive/Getty Images
Page 156 Album/Alamy Stock Photo
Pages 158-159 Ernst Haas/Getty Images
Page 160 Ernst Haas/Getty Images
Page 161 Ernst Haas/Getty Images
Pages 162-163 Ernst Haas/Getty Images
Page 163 Ernst Haas/Getty Images
Page 164 John Kobal Foundation/Getty Images
Page 165 Ernst Haas/Getty Images
Page 166 Lawrence Schiller/Getty Images
Page 169 Bettmann/Getty Images
Page 170 Kena Betancur/Getty Images
Page 171 ZUMA Press, Inc./Alamy Stock Photo
Page 173 Donaldson Collection/Getty Images
Page 174 Michael Ochs Archives/Getty Images
Page 175 Album/Alamy Stock Photo
Page 176 Bill Waterson/Alamy Stock Photo
Page 177 Bill Waterson/Alamy Stock Photo
Page 178 ullstein bild Dtl./Getty Images
Page 179 Bettmann/Getty Images
Page 180 Hulton Archive/Getty Images
Page 181 Pictorial Press Ltd/Alamy Stock Photo
Page 182 Bettmann/Getty Images
Page 183 Bettmann/Getty Images
Page 184 Album/Alamy Stock Photo
Page 185 Sports Studio Photos/Getty Images
Page 186 Bettmann/Getty Images
Page 187 JJs/Alamy Stock Photo
Page 189 PictureLux/The Hollywood Archive/Alamy Stock Photo
Page 190 Archive Photos/Getty Images
Pages 192-193 Harold Clements/Getty Images
Page 194 Smith Archive/Alamy Stock Photo
Page 195 Slade Paul/Getty Images
Page 196 Paul Schutzer/Getty Images
Page 197 PictureLux/The Hollywood Archive/Alamy Stock Photo
Page 198 Bob Haswell/Getty Images
Page 199 Bettmann/Getty Images
Page 200 New York Daily News Archive/Getty Images
Page 201 PictureLux/The Hollywood Archive/Alamy Stock Photo
Page 202 Archive Photos/Getty Images
Page 203 Screen Archives/Getty Images
Pages 204-205 Hulton Archive/Getty Images
Page 206 Michael Ochs Archives/Getty Images
Page 208 Bettmann/Getty Images
Page 209 Moviestore Collection Ltd/Alamy Stock Photo
Page 211 Bettmann/Getty Images
Page 213 PictureLux/The Hollywood Archive/Alamy Stock Photo
Page 215 Michael Ochs Archives/Getty Images
Page 219 Bettmann/Getty Images
Pages 220-221 Hulton Archive

Cover: Baron/Stringer/Getty Images

Editorial Project
Consulting D&D/Valeria Manferto De Fabianis

Graphic Layout
Maria Cucchi

WS whitestar™ is a trademark property of White Star s.r.l.

Piazzale Luigi Cadorna, 6
20123 Milan, Italy
www.whitestar.it

Translation: Irina Oryschevic – Editing: Abby Young

ISBN 978-88-544-2155-4
1 2 3 4 5 6 29 28 27 26 25

Printed in China